Look at Me!

Look at Me!

The Fame Motive from Childhood to Death

Orville Gilbert Brim

The University of Michigan Press ☆ *Ann Arbor*

Copyright © by the University of Michigan 2009
All rights reserved
Published in the United States of America by
The University of Michigan Press
Manufactured in the United States of America
♾ Printed on acid-free paper

2012   2011   2010   2009   4   3   2   1

A CIP catalog record for this book is available from the British Library.

Library of Congress Cataloging-in-Publication Data

Brim, Orville Gilbert, 1923–
    Look at me! : the fame motive from childhood to death / Orville
Gilbert Brim.
        p.   cm.
    Includes bibliographical references.
    ISBN 978-0-472-07070-1 (cloth : alk. paper) — ISBN 978-0-472-
05070-3 (pbk. : alk. paper)
    1. Fame.   2. Fame—Psychological aspects.   I. Title.
BJ1470.5.B75   2009
153.8—dc22   2009018637

TO KATHY ☆ *my beloved life companion for sixty years*

Acknowledgments

I thank my many friends who helped in the creation of this book by giving steady encouragement, by reading various drafts along the way and responding with honest comments and usable suggestions, and by often providing an apt word or sentence.

Contents

Introduction

Four million adults in the United States say that becoming famous is the most important goal in their lives. In any random group of one hundred American adults, two will have fame as their consuming desire. This book is about these unusual people among us who are trying to achieve fame and then trying to stay famous if they do. How did they get that way? Where did the motivation come from? What is the influence of the desire for fame on their personalities? How is it expressed during their lives, and what happens to them as their lives unfold?

Fame

When a world champion marathon runner from Ethiopia said, "I want to be famous; I want people to talk about me," he described the basic meaning of fame. To be famous means that, somewhere, many people whom you do not know are thinking about you and talking about you. Over the centuries, medallions and coins, sculpture, painted portraits, printed words, photographs, radio, film, television, and the Internet have expanded the original meaning of fame far beyond "many people talking about you." Now you can be famous because you've made news and many people are reading about you, or you're being interviewed on national television, or you're in a public place and people recognize you and even ask for your autograph. Fame now may include face and voice as well as name. If you're famous, you may be recognized for one, two, or even all three of these. (See "Etymology of the Word *Fame*.")

What qualifies a person as famous? How well known must he or she be? "Well known?" a friend asked me dismissively. "Well known is not famous. Fame is being on the front page of the *New York Times*." Everyone is talked about by others, ranging in numbers from a handful of people, to small and larger groups, to the nation and the world. When this recognition goes beyond one's family and neighborhood and workplace—beyond the primary in-groups who can appreciate one's achievements—to include people one does not know, one can be considered famous. Fame is recognition by strangers. Two flight attendants on a flight from Boston to Los Angeles said the "famous" are the people they know from their names on the passenger list.

In this book, fame is loosely defined: people are famous when known by name, recognized by sight, and talked about or written about by a nameless public unknown to them. There is also a legal concept of fame, that of the "public figure." Among the evidence a court will consider in determining whether a person is indeed a public figure are name-recognition statistics, a degree of media coverage prior to the case, and degree of access to the media. If a person or group has taken steps to attract public attention and in some measure done so, such as by appearing twice on the *Today Show*, a court will view them as public figures.

Fame is also a matter of degree. In the United States, there is the Shuffleboard Hall of Fame and the Baseball Hall of Fame. Those enshrined in the former don't qualify as famous—few of us would know who they are—while those in the Baseball Hall of Fame clearly do. Appraisals of fame include how many people know of you and how often your name comes up in conversations, in how many different parts of society and in how many countries. It's been said that the highest level of fame is when lunatics believe they are you, especially when—like Jesus, Napoleon, or Hitler—you are dead.

The Purpose of This Book

My aim in this book is to describe the origin and life course of the human desire for fame. Many books have been published about fame itself, including advice on how to become famous, descriptions of famous persons, a history of fame through the ages, a sociological analysis of prestige, an economic analysis of the value of fame to society, and collections of naked pictures of the famous, as well as compilations about wives or children of the famous, intimate sex lives of the famous, and how the famous died and the locations of their graves.[1] In contrast, we have only a few commentaries on the fame *motive*. It remains relatively unexamined by scholars who study human personality and human development. They have been more interested in the motivations for power, sex, and money; the urge to create art and literature; and the need to search for knowledge or express love of country.

Most personality characteristics can be measured by scientific tests. There are no tests for the fame motive, however; nor are there any experiments or field studies through which it can be objectively appraised and then related to childhood or adolescent experiences. Likewise nonexistent are the reverse: studies that appraise childhood experiences of people and then track their attitudes toward fame through midlife and old age, measuring any changes.

I am a social psychologist who can point to a lifetime of scholarly achievement that includes considerable research on human personality development. But this book is not a scientific study, nor is it meant to be a popular or self-help book. It is, rather, an extended essay about one aspect of human nature. I've pondered the nature of the fame motive for years, and what follows are the impressions, speculations, and assertions refined from my thinking over those years. Owing to the absence of scholarly studies, I've had few scientific facts to work with. Hence my thoughts and conclusions are mainly derived from readings and personal interviews. The respondents include social and behavioral scientists, of course, but many other occupations as well, diversified by age and gender. Also, I've had many opportunities over the years to observe and listen to people as they aspire to fame. And because I myself am one of the four million who long for fame, this is in part a personal narrative of my own struggles and experiences with the fame motive.

Two Basic Distinctions

Let me start by setting up two guideposts. First, I've often been asked, "What about people who are very good at something and merely want to be recognized for their skill and hard work?" Attempts to achieve excellence, on the one hand, and fame, on the other, may be much the same; it's the target audience that makes the difference. There is indeed a fundamental difference—one that will be cited often in this book—between the wish to be recognized and honored by a group of peers, which is not fame, and the wish to be recognized and honored by persons whom one does not know, which is the essence of fame.

A comparison of two scientists illustrates this difference. The first, Huxley, is seeking not fame but the "reassurance" of fellow members of the Royal Society. The second, the physicist Silverman, wants recognition and discussion about himself beyond "friends and colleagues"—that is, fame. Robert K. Merton says,

> The function of reassurance by recognition has a dependable basis in the social aspects of knowledge. Few scientists have great certainty about the worth of their work . . . Even that psychological stalwart, T. H. Huxley, seemingly the acme of self-confidence, tells in his diary what it meant to him to be elected to the Royal Society at the age of 26 . . . It provided him, above all, with much needed reassurance that he was on the right track.[2]

In his study of the ambitions of scientists, Joseph C. Hermanowicz writes,

> We see the image of a future self in the account of Geoff Silverman. Silverman, who is at midcareer, eloquently describes an identity he hopes to assume by demonstrating scientific prowess. "The dream is to discover some fantastic new effect that knocks the socks off my friends and colleagues, that knocks the socks off the community, so that when I walk down the corridor, the young students . . . say, 'There goes [Silverman], he invented the [Silverman] effect.'"[3]

A second question frequently asked is, "Don't people want fame for a variety of reasons?" The answer is, "Yes, of course," and this question itself points up the fundamental distinction between the fame motive's primary and secondary forms. The primary form, analyzed in this book, arises from a basic human need for acceptance and approval by others and from rejection by other persons and groups. One seeks to become famous in order to compensate for the acceptance and approval that others have withheld. In contrast, fame obviously can help greatly in achieving a variety of goals in life, such as money, power, good works, and more (see chap. 4). When fame is less an end in itself than a means of reaching other objectives, the fame motive appears in its secondary form.

Part One ☆ **Understanding the Motive**

1 ☆ The Nature of the Fame Motive

The Need to Belong

Psychologists who study personality make lists of human motives, but, surprisingly, the fame motive does not appear on anyone's list. Nor is the word *fame* indexed in any of the leading texts on personality development, in comprehensive books on human motivation, or in edited volumes or handbooks describing personality and/or social psychology. It is also not in *The International Handbook of Psychology* or in the eight-volume *Encyclopedia of Psychology.*

True, some well-known psychologists, such as William James, mention the gregarious nature of humans, referring to the "need to belong," the desire to be with others and be accepted by them.[1] Henry Murray's list of "needs" (drives) is close to the topic. The list includes "To make an impression. To be seen and heard. To excite, amaze, fascinate, entertain, shock, intrigue, amuse, or entice others." A sample, self-descriptive item reads, "I am apt to show off in some way if I get a chance." Also, a "drive for recognition": "that is, a desire to excite praise and commendation, to demand respect, social approval and prestige, honors and fame."[2] Neither James nor Murray goes beyond these descriptions, however, to identify a motive for fame, or consider its development through life.

I believe that people with the desire for fame are not born with the motive but acquire it during life. Edmund Burke, a great English statesman, in his "speech on American Taxation" said that "passion for fame" is "a passion which is the instinct of all great souls." But this is not true. The motive is not an instinct. It is learned. It originates in the human need for acceptance and approval.

Evolutionary psychologists have long asserted that human survival depends on belonging to social groups. They explain that "children . . . would be more likely to survive . . . because of the care they receive" and that "the likely result of this evolutionary selection would be a set of internal mechanisms that guide individuals . . . into social groups."[3] Group cooperation provides food and safety.

Psychologists who study child development describe, in a thousand studies, how children associate the satisfaction of basic needs, such as hunger and warmth, with the approving and accepting presence of another human, at first almost always the mother. The child comes to recognize that meeting basic needs is dependent on the favorable judgment of others and that this approval is contingent on his or her own behavior. From the very first instance of a parent's saying, "You ought to be ashamed of yourself," the child can recognize that approval brings love, affection, nurture, relief from anxiety, pleasure, even exhilaration; conversely, disapproval brings rejection, withdrawal of support, even punishment. Evidence suggests a general conclusion that being accepted, included, or welcomed leads to a variety of positive emotions (e.g., happiness, elation, contentment, and calm), whereas being rejected, excluded, or ignored leads to potent negative feelings (e.g., anxiety, depression, grief, jealousy, and loneliness).[4]

The Fame Motive as a Consequence of Rejection

We all need the knowledge that we're loved, supported, approved of, and accepted by others—the inner assurance that allows us to say, "I am secure; I do belong; I am safe here." For most people, these needs are satisfied within the intimate circles of parents, family, friends, and the other small groups to which one belongs. But for some of us, this never happens. One can feel excluded for a variety of reasons. The consequence of being rejected by parents, especially a mother, is the most studied. Emotional or physical abandonment or simply lack of approval and security will cause anxiety, distress, and fear in the infant, leading to a basic insecurity that becomes part of the infant's developing sense of self. To this base may be added the loss of one or both parents, sibling rivalry and defeat, exclusion from the adolescent peer group because of physical or personality defects, or refusal by possible marriage partners due to different moral or cultural values. Later in life, one may experience divorce, rejection by one's children, or estrangement at the workplace.

Studies of the outcomes of such rejections cite anxiety, fear, distorted thinking, even mental illness. More recently, experiments in neuroscience reveal that social exclusion actually creates physical distress. Functional magnetic resonance imaging shows that excluded persons have a pattern of brain activities and blood-flow changes similar to those of people suffering bodily pain.

To be rejected by persons and groups close to us creates a sense of being unloved and unwanted. This sparks the fame motive. The yearning to belong—somewhere—causes us to seek fulfillment through the attention and approval of strangers. Fame is expected to bring the comfort and assurance that comes from being wanted, accepted, even admired. We become driven to find audiences whose response to us is positive, so that we can simply leave behind those who rejected us, saying with confidence (if only to ourselves), "I don't need you, others will have me, you were wrong," as increasingly we're talked about, read about, seen, and recognized by a number of people far exceeding the number of those who rejected us.

One must quickly set some limits on this generalization. Everyone has experienced some rejection by others, causing mild insecurity, but seldom with lasting effects. It is multiple experiences of rejection and their intensity and duration, especially when young, that cause one to feel unwanted and unloved.

It is also not inevitable that being rejected triggers a desire for fame. Sigmund Freud cautions,

> So long as we trace development from its final outcome backwards, the chain of events appears continuous and we feel we have gained an insight which is completely satisfactory, and even exhaustive. But, if we proceed the reverse way, if we start from the premises inferred from the analysis and try to follow these up to the final result, then we no longer get the impression of an inevitable sequence of events which could not have been otherwise determined. We notice at once that there might have been another result, and that we might have been just as well able to understand and explain the latter . . . Hence the chain of causation can always be recognized with certainty if we follow the line of analysis [backward] whereas to predict . . . is impossible.[5]

For those who suffer from lack of acceptance and approval or feel estranged from other human beings, fame is only one of many possible compensations. Some will find acceptance in the love of God. Others will find it through the deep and unconditional love of another person. A few will have animals that love them. There are also the considerations of losing oneself in one's work or a personal passion, such as a social cause or collecting first editions. Tragically, however, some to whom the thought of fame as a possible remedy for their inner distress never occurs—or, worse, who never find a way to ease the feelings of loneliness and inadequacy within their secret selves—will suffer as long as they live.

Instances

The diverse cases that follow illustrate the range and variety of experiences that give rise to the fame motive. In a rare description of its origin, Sue Erickson Bloland, herself a psychoanalyst, writes about her famous father, Erik Erickson,

> My father never knew his father, or even who his father was. One of the saddest things about that, from my point of view, is that his mother refused throughout her life to tell him the identity of this all-important person . . . My father's drive to become famous may well have been, at least in part, an effort to win on a wide scale the attention and admiration that he could not obtain from his father . . . [F]rom early childhood on I was aware that his drive to achieve recognition was monumental.[6]

Jonathan Adler, a clinical psychologist, writes about another famous person, the celebrity-singer Madonna. When she was six years old, her mother died, and her father married one of the family's housekeepers. After graduating from high school, Madonna went to New York at age nineteen, with thirty-five dollars in her pocket. She spent five years working at a variety of jobs, from coat checker at the Russian Tea Room to nude model for budding photographers. Adler quotes Madonna: "I think that when you grow up without a mother, as I did, you have a real sort of unfulfilled need inside yourself and are in a mad search for love. I also think you carry around a kind of unspoken despair . . . When my mother died, all of a sudden I was going to become the best—the best singer, the best dancer, the most famous person in the world. Everybody was going to love me."[7]

When the well-known comic author and columnist Art Buchwald was asked about his career, he replied, "The whole point with me is that I didn't have any love from home, so I got it all from the crowd. It's the story of a lot of creative people who want applause."[8]

Although the absence of acceptance and approval seems most damaging when it occurs within the family during infancy and childhood, rejection by people outside the family later on can also generate a powerful desire to be famous. Juliet Macur describes the youth of Terrell Owens, a famous show-off and professional football player for the Dallas Cowboys: "He was picked on, beat up, laughed at, . . . the clumsy kid chosen last for the team . . . 'If you saw what he looked like back then, you would have wanted to beat him up too,' said . . . one of Owens' neighborhood friends. 'He was like a little geek.'"[9] Andy Warhol, known for his art, photography, and film and for the saying "In the future everybody will be world-famous for fifteen minutes" was said to be a publicity hound and "the diabolically clever author of his own celebrity."[10] Born in Pittsburgh to a working-class Czech family, Warhol suffered from the nervous disorder St. Vitus's dance when he was a boy, which accounted for his strange pallor, his blotchy skin, and his shyness. He was taunted as "Spot" by his schoolmates.

As for myself, motivated by fame throughout a long life, I had a truly strange childhood. My parents were quite old and my mother was ill much of the time. My parents also were not close and I had little guidance from either of them in my childhood. I hardly saw and never really knew my three older sisters—they were mystery sisters. I was brought up, in fact, mostly by cousins, a series of farm children who came to live with us while they went to Ohio State University in Columbus, Ohio.

I grew up in Columbus during the 1930s and went to a "university school" across town, so I didn't know children in my neighborhood to make friends with. During summers, the family vacationed in an isolated cottage among the giant pines and hemlocks of Lake Winnipesaukee in New Hampshire. When I was ten and eleven years old, I would take the streetcar by myself out to the southwest part of Columbus to watch the Redbirds (the St. Louis Cardinals' minor-league baseball team). After school, I would sit alone with my dog and read. I would turn on the radio for Jack Armstrong's adventures at five o'clock or sometimes listen to a ball game. To a degree unusual in children, I spent my days alone.

In those years, the smart child was advanced in school to whatever level of work he or she could handle. Nowadays, advanced pupils are kept with their age-group in special classes, but there were no such classes back then.

I skipped not one but two grades. I was two years younger than the others in my class and was treated accordingly. My looks were weird as well. For years, I wore glasses, then thought to be sissified and barring one from most sports. I also had facial tics and neck twitches, earning me the nickname "Twertch"—a combination of the words *twitch* and *twerp*. I had to endure repeated cruelties of ridicule and rejection, many of which I still recall.

Among older children, recent research on sibling violence and school bullying—threats, ridicule, name-calling, hitting, slapping, and other forms of intimidation and harassment—reports that in large-scale national studies, 35 percent of children had been hit or attacked by a sibling in the previous year.[11] In a second study, 10 percent of students reported that they had been bullied "sometimes or weekly." Research indicates that victims of this persistent mistreatment—being picked on and even beaten by their more powerful peers—"suffer various symptoms of psychological distress, such as depression, anxiety, and loneliness."[12] Many people have questioned whether the widespread coverage of school violence by local and even national media has increased its occurrence. The answer is probably yes, in that the publicity demonstrates to school-age adolescents how one can achieve recognition and thus opens a new path to becoming famous—or infamous.

The massacre of students at Virginia Tech in 2007 and the Colorado school killings—the "Columbine Massacre"—in 1999 show how the fame motive can emerge from postchildhood rejection. In the case of the Colorado killings, the two teenagers had been ridiculed and made fun of and abused by other teenagers. There was more there than anger. They were after fame.[13] Seung-Hui Cho, the murderer at Virginia Tech, was silent and withdrawn most of the time as a child in Seoul: "He was scrawny and looked younger than his age. He was unresponsive in class, and unwilling to speak . . . Classmates recall some teasing and bullying over his taciturn nature."[14] At Virginia Tech, he hated the other students. Before the massacre, he put together a package of photographs and videos of himself, together with a statement and a suicide note, and sent it by overnight mail to NBC. It was displayed the next day on NBC television.

In later years, one can be abandoned or divorced by a spouse, fired from work, avoided by former friends because of some foolish or deviant action, ostracized because of race or ethnicity or gender, or shunned as a pariah by the community. Experiences of rejection like these, any of them capable of igniting the fame motive, not only may occur in adult life but, for some, may be repeated through the years and cumulative in their effect. The same person may be rejected in infancy by the mother, unloved as a child, an outcast from an adolescent peer group, and excluded from the adult community—experiencing a never-ending frustration to the need to be accepted and a continuing assault on one's sense of self-worth.

Self-Images of Future Fame

The concept of self is something of an enigma—certainly complex and extremely hard to define. In *The Oxford English Dictionary*, three and a half pages are devoted to the single word *self*, which goes back to primordial times. Today, scientists assume that self-awareness is a natural feature of brain matter—something we don't yet understand and, some say, probably never will.

Contemplate a child's first contact with the phenomenon of fame. How and at what age does the idea of being known to a lot of other people—people the child doesn't know—first occur? Not until the ages of five, six, or seven can a child engage in thinking in the abstract. Before then, the child can understand whether people value and admire him or her if they are people he or she knows and/or can see. What is not yet possible is thinking about people in general, unknown to the child. Only later will the child develop images of fame: what it is, what it may mean, how it may occur.

Evidence that the concept of fame is increasingly understood as a child grows older appears in a 1989 survey of three thousand children in the United States. The survey began with the question "Which one of the following do you think will be MOST important to you as you face the future?" Seven possible answers were presented, including "becoming a famous or important person." The second question asked, "Which one of the following do you think will be LEAST important?" The number of children saying that becoming famous was most important to them increased from 8 percent in grades 4–6 to 43 percent for grades 7–12, and the numbers saying "least important" increased from 7 percent for grades 4–6 to 53 percent for grades 7–12.[15]

These comparisons by age strongly suggest that as children grow older, they are able to understand the substance of the questions, that is, the meaning of fame. They also suggest that something new and different occurs around the age of ten in some children. They begin to create images of themselves. The images may be of a past self, a present self, a possible self, a fantasy self, a lost and regretted self, or a future self. My interest, of course, is in the developing sense of self in terms of being liked or dis-liked—whether one is lovable or unloved, unaccepted, unapproved. This latter sense of self leads directly to the fame motive and the attempt to ef-face one's shaming self-image by creating a new one founded on the fa-mous future self.

In most families and schools, there is little discussion about fame. As with other sensitive subjects not usually talked about, such as sex, the im-age one has of oneself in relation to fame will be fuzzy and unclear. This is the case in the following letter from a teenage girl.

> I want to be famous. I guess you can say I'm an average fifteen-year-old girl: stubborn and witty, but shy and introverted. I have a low self-es-teem, and I'm often depressed. I am 5'3", skinny, tan, and unappealing, with shoulder-length brown hair, big brown eyes, and an oblong face. I don't have many friends (any more), but events in my past lead me to realize that quality is better than quantity. I am an elite runner, I play the flute, I love art, and I have plenty of free time (as you can tell). I love tropical weather, but I live in New York (go figure). I wish I were famous. Enough about me, though . . .
>
> In my case, the desire for fame is bad. I want something that could never be, I'm not a good actress, I'm not a good singer, and I'm not a beautiful, anorexic, 5'10" girl with the potential of being a model. I don't take any acting courses. I don't try, because I know how hard it is to get "in."
>
> It is said that everyone will get their fifteen minutes of fame. It is also said that one out of four people will be on TV at one point in their lives. So you basically have a 25 percent chance of getting your fifteen minutes of fame. For an unlucky person like me, it is doubtful that I will ever get my fifteen minutes of fame.
>
> I don't share my desire for fame with anyone—not my parents, not my siblings, not my friends. It's kind of like an inner secret with myself. It's like a dream that will never come true. I often try to forget about it, since I don't want to be disappointed. But you never know . . . Maybe one day you'll see me on TV, in the papers and magazines. Hey, any-thing is possible.

Beyond our inner selves, however, our culture surrounds us with repre-sentations of fame and famous people. Says a friend, "Was there ever a thirteen-year-old boy who participated in sports who didn't fantasize about leaping up against the wall and catching a fly ball and becoming famous? Or hitting a home run in the bottom of the ninth with the bases loaded?" Images of fame seem to be everywhere. Another friend offers a vignette of his granddaughter. At ten or eleven, she applied to a special school for the performing arts and was interviewed as to her interest. "I told them ballet and singing," she said, "because someday I'm going to be famous, and I'd better get good at something."

Personally, I doubt if many self-images emerge at such an early age. Those that do, based on dreams and fantasies, will probably change—with more durable images of future fame appearing only later. In my own instance, the image of myself as a famous writer came into being, I think, when I was twelve years old and had won a contest selling magazines door-to-door. The prize was a book of my choice, and I selected Tolstoy's *War and Peace,* knowing nothing about it except that it was important. When the package bearing it arrived by mail, it was addressed to me, and because it was a package, the postman brought it to the front door, rang the doorbell, and handed it to me. It was the first mail I had ever received. I opened the package to see the impressive tan-and-brown volume (the Modern Library edition), and it dawned on me that there was a world of books and authors and readers "out there" that I would like to be part of.

An interesting comparison of images of future fame emerges from three surveys dated from 1987–97. A group of respondents who admitted to daydreaming about being famous were asked to choose what kind of person they would most like to be from a list of fifteen possibilities (see "What Kind of Famous Person Would You Most Like to Be?"). The list included such famous types (listed here by percentage of respondents who chose them) as an author of best-selling books (15), a popular singer (15), a sports star in a team sport (14), a movie actor or actress (11), a high-ranking businessperson (13), a famous scientist (7), and a high-ranking government official (7).

Over the ten-year period, the surveys recorded stability in the rankings of the types just listed. What stands out is the large and statistically significant difference in the number of respondents who subsequently rejected all of them. The number who responded "None of these" rose from 18 to 31 percent.[16] To explain this shift, one can only speculate. My own guess is that during the ten years of the surveys, additional "famous" occupations with which the respondents could identify emerged, probably owing to an increased focus on celebrities in the media. Concurrently, previously obscure pursuits, such as protecting the environment or crusading for a minority or against a disease, began attracting public attention and the fame potential that goes with it.

The self-image of future fame envisioned by a medical researcher striving for a Nobel Prize will of course differ from the self-image of an aspiring actress striving for an Academy Award. Yet the fame they experience—if they do—may be quite similar. An observant friend cautions,

> A Nobel Prize winner and this season's winner on *Survivor* don't become famous for the same reasons, and their contributions to society are incredibly different, but I'm not sure that their fame is significantly different. To me, one of the most interesting criticisms of our media-saturated culture is that fame has been democratized, for better or worse, and so a psychologist who revolutionized modern economic theory (Daniel Kanneman, a Nobel Prize recipient) and the random person who triumphed on *Survivor* (who knows, who cares?) both get to make it into the *New York Times* and onto the *Today Show*. In other words, while some people become famous for reasons of substance and others achieve fame by accident or through luck or guile, I think that the fame they experience is analogous. To most people they're primarily celebrities and therefore equal.

Not everyone motivated by fame will have this future self-image. Some may pursue fame but not be aware that this is their motive. They may be ignorant of the fact that they are seeking fame (as I say in chapter 2). They may think that what they are doing is for some other reason. If someone wants to be famous to fulfill the need for approval but is not aware or denies that this is happening, I understand there will be no image of oneself as famous. The actual goal being sought is never imagined and perhaps never really understood by such a person.

A Never-Ending Desire

As with other learned motives—power, money, good works—the fame motive can be denied, repressed, even consciously abhorred in oneself. It can be in conflict with other motives or in a synergistic relationship with them. It can serve as a means of achieving goals that satisfy other motives. It can be aroused and intensified by rejection. It can be strong or weak. As it develops, the motive can be hidden. Although it can exist in latent form—"present or potential but not evident or active"—a wounding event of exclusion or rejection in midlife or earlier, superimposed on the vulnerability sustained in childhood or adolescence, can reinvigorate the motive, just as the chickenpox suffered in childhood may reappear in times of stress later on as the nervous affliction shingles.

So, one may ask, is the fame motive ever satisfied? Are people motivated by fame ever content with the fame they manage to achieve—for a day, a month, or even a lifetime—or do they keep needing more? Does the motive gradually ebb through a life span as the person accumulates small, passing experiences of fame? Do cumulative social insults and rejections through a life span cause the motive to increase? We don't yet know. Presumably, a person with a moderate motive for fame would be satisfied with moderate fame. But what is satisfaction? It may be that a small reward only increases the desire for more. We know, for example, that in studies of income, people say that just having 25 percent more coming in would be enough for them—and they say this regardless of their income level. Can't it be that the desire for fame and the desire for money are twins?

In my view, based on my own experience, the fame motive will not go away but must be endured as a kind of chronic hunger, never completely satisfied for the rest of one's life. To illustrate, I lately came across some notes from a journal I kept when in my early twenties. I had just failed to receive a much-coveted job offer and was trying to remake my personality, especially by ridding myself of the fame motive.

> I felt then, and I know now, that I cannot go through this again. I have talked often to myself of a time like this, the many truths to be faced, and the trauma it may induce. I know also that I do not want to go on living with the strain toward achievement which I have had. The hollowness of all victories of this type is patent—consider the logical result of this insatiable pursuit. I must solve this problem now of the desire for fame, so that I need to disavow the motive to not have such events in the future. I can have no rational basis for the desire for fame; it is a stranger to my ethic. I cannot justify to myself this desire, and I cannot live with myself when I have it. I think I can start deliberately toning down this need. I must view my work in terms of its contribution to the good for society, rather than the achievement of fame . . .
>
> It is more of a rearrangement of the values of the goals, a changing of priorities. Note that this does not mean one must not work hard. It means rather that one should work hard for the good. The harder the

better, in fact. More power to the energetic man. Such work may well bring recognition or renown. However, the point is that one must guard against the slipping over of the goal into the sphere of fame, rather than the good.

My struggle is obvious, reflecting how difficult it is to extinguish or redirect a motive that is embedded in one's personality, probably at a deep level, and how a rational effort to change may be countered by a verbal cleverness designed to make it seem that change has occurred without much actually happening.

The notes continue,

> For myself, I am aware that the diminishing of my desire for recognition is still going on; it seems to be switching over from a desire to be "a great man in the field" to a desire to "make a great contribution." Perhaps this may be only playing with words on my part, casting a different tone over my activities; if true, it represents a step toward unification of desires. Certainly, I tend to think more now in terms of great contribution than great man.

We see here an attempt to change without really changing, to camouflage the desire for recognition by giving it a new name, "desire to make a great contribution." During the next several years, my struggle to abandon the goal of fame continued or, rather, shifted to "doing good" (through research in psychology).

Meanwhile, I seem to have been considering another way to nullify the fame motive by adopting still another goal, that of "making a difference." I wrote (youthful thoughts),

> About age 30 a transformation is likely to occur consisting of a change from name-fame to anonymous immortality. People learn from experience, from history, from science fiction, that names are not remembered for the most part, no matter how well known the contribution might be during the actual lifetime or in fact how significant it is in substance. Looking for immortality, they recognize no immortality of name. A change then takes place. The person's goal interest shifts to contributions to the future course of mankind and the immortality of having some influence carried forever as part of man's heritage. The name of the person disappears but the influence remains, not displaced

by newer ideas, more certain knowledge, the next social revolution, but rather that these build upon what came before. Thus every new book, new discovery, new society, carries the contributions of those of the past as well as those of the present. But for them, mankind would be different. And so they say that one who contributes in this way to the course of human evolution is immortal.

At that point, I wanted to contribute to the well-being of humanity, but note how the fame motive sneaked back in. Now I seek assurance that my contribution—that is, my achievement—would be important. Since I also wanted to free myself from any connection between the value of my work and the fame it might bring, I left everything to the judgments of people in the future, thinking that they might well recognize the contribution I hoped to make even though it went unnoticed then.

Finally, I wrote,

Who can foresee what quietly and subtly planted seed, now unrecognized, will grow in value in centuries later. Conversely, others may become famous and achieve eminence but they have given little to later ages and therefore all they have disappears with their death.

Here is a clever, self-protective rationalization. Although I couldn't prove I was right about how things would work out, no one else could prove me wrong.

Being convinced that the fame motive is never satisfied and never disappears, I believe that while it may weaken through life, it also may strengthen, stimulated by fresh instances of exclusion in adulthood. Seeking examples of this, I wrote to a number of psychologists who study motivation. I asked them, "What do people do when they see that their motive for fame is not going to be satisfied? Viewing the motive as insatiable, I have searched for studies or reports on attempts to rid oneself of it in adult life, when many seek fame through accumulation of money, power, good works, et al. Thousands of studies of changing behavior exist, as with losing weight, giving up alcohol and so on, but I find nothing about abandoning the pursuit of fame. Is mine the only inquiry of fame as a motive throughout the life span? Can you advise?" None of my correspondents could give me a single reference.

The fame motive's insatiability makes for a sad story. Although individuals may believe fame to be the answer to their unfulfilled need for approval and acceptance, it will never, in fact, fully satisfy their longing. This conclusion is based on my own observations and the assertions of others who share it. A perceptive former colleague observes, "Fame, recognition, and acknowledgment feel great to the ego and boost your self-esteem but are not the same as love, acceptance, and safety, although we pursue fame as if it will give us these things."

The following is from my interview with a distinguished psychologist (a woman in midlife).

> *I was going to ask you to name some people with a passion for fame.*
>
> [name of person]. Off the charts. He comes to mind immediately; he might be the archetype of the pursuit of fame. I'm assuming you're not going to use these names.
>
> *Certainly not.*
>
> And my colleague at [work] . . . is also off the charts. I don't find him quite as offensive.
>
> In all of these people . . . the pursuit is fundamentally rooted in a deep sense of personal insecurity. And that is fueled by a kind of constant need for applause that can never truly minister to the inner sense of inadequacy. And I don't even think people always have a conscious awareness of all these things.

Sue Erikson Bloland says, "We want to believe that if we ourselves could just secure enough recognition and approval from the outside world, if we could feel sufficiently admired, we would be healed and our self-esteem secured." She concludes, "And, of course, my parents did enjoy many advantages and pleasures as a result of Dad's celebrity. But what was concealed behind their glowing public image was a sad reality: that fame had not healed their early childhood wounds."[17]

Summary

- The origin of the fame motive is in the basic human need for acceptance and approval.
- When this need is not fulfilled because of rejection by parents or adolescent peer groups or others, basic insecurity develops and emerges as the fame motive.

- Persons with the fame motive will have self-images of future fame; the content may change, but there will always be an image of some kind.
- The fame motive continues through life. Even though fame is not the answer to the unmet need for love and acceptance, the desire for fame remains, driven by that basic need.

2 ☆ Millions of People Want Fame

In the United States

In chapter 1, I asserted that four million American adults say that fame is their most important life goal. This conclusion is based on the findings of more than a dozen national attitude and opinion surveys that asked about fame. They were conducted by several different organizations, and the data are stored in the archives of the Roper Center for Public Opinion Research in Storrs, Connecticut. The results were sent to me by the archivists at the Roper Center for inclusion in this book. The analysis of the findings is my own.

In several of these surveys, the respondents were required to choose among a number of life goals, including becoming famous. A caution is necessary here: except for either-or ultimatums, such as "Give up drinking or give up me," forced choices are rare in life, and forced choices among a variety of values are rarer still. One might be skeptical, therefore, about the findings of forced-choice surveys that include fame. It's therefore reassuring to learn that the surveys considered in this chapter, though conducted at sometimes widely differing dates, are surprisingly alike in their findings about Americans' attitudes toward fame.

Fame: The Most Important Goal in Life

When surveys require that a choice be made among life goals, fame does not rank high. One survey that is an exception, almost certainly because it forced the respondent to make an either-or choice, asked, "Would you rather be famous or in love?" In that survey, 75 percent of respondents chose love, while 20 percent said they would rather be famous.[1] Nearly all other surveys I considered offered multiple choices and produced quite different findings. One asked, "Which one of the following factors would most give you the feeling of success in life?" "A happy family life" led the list of six alternatives, being chosen by 62 percent of respondents. "Fame" came in last, at only 1 percent.[2] Two other surveys asked about importance. "What is most important to you—fame, money, career, sex, or marriage?" asked one, with "fame" named by 3 percent of respondents. The other asked, "Which of the following personal traits do you want most . . . intelligence, courage, beauty, wealth, or fame?" "Fame" was named by 1 percent of respondents.[3]

In three national surveys of adults (in 1989, 1990, and 1996), the *Los Angeles Times* asked, "What would you say is your main goal in life: is it to be successful in a career, or to raise children, or to be famous, or to be happily married, or to help others, or to have power?" In all three surveys, the choices "children" and "happily married" together were selected by 95 percent of respondents. Being famous was chosen by 1 percent.[4]

In a 1975 interview, the respondents were given a card that listed some basic goals in life and were then asked, "People have different ideas about what it means to be successful. Which one or two things on this card come closest to expressing your personal idea of success?" In 1985, the survey was repeated. In both instances, "being prominent or famous" was selected by 3 percent of the respondents.[5]

Taken together, these national surveys indicate that 1–3 percent of Americans rank becoming famous as their most important life goal. In the United States, there are more than two hundred million noninstitutionalized persons aged twenty or over.[6] One percent of the two hundred million persons is two million, and 3 percent is six million. Averaging the two percentages produces a total of four million people as a reasonable estimate of how widespread the fame motive is in the U.S. population—roughly 2 percent. Compare the incidence of some common life-threatening illnesses:[7] stroke, 2.4 percent; chronic bronchitis, 4.4 percent; emphysema, 1.5 percent; female breast cancer, 2 percent; male prostate cancer, 1.5 percent; kidney disease, 1.3 percent; and liver disease, 1.4 percent.

A more recent set of findings makes me think that the 2 percent estimate for the fame motive may be on the low side. A national survey conducted in 2006 asked people aged 18–39, "Which of the following do you think people in your generation or age-group think is most important? . . . To get rich, to be famous, to help people who need help, to be leaders in their community, to become more spiritual." "Getting rich" was the most frequent answer (55 percent), but 8 percent said "to be famous."[8] This higher percentage is probably explained by the absence in a respondent universe of people over forty, for whom fame may seem a fading possibility. What about the people for whom becoming famous isn't a primary goal but is still an important one—say number two or three? If the surveys had probed that deep, I believe that the number of those for whom fame is an objective of more than fleeting importance would increase by many millions.

Is the indicated incidence of the fame motive a lot or a little? Unfortunately, there are no other studies that describe the incidence of a motive in a population group. Types of motivation are surely distributed in some ways in populations. I would compare the incidence of the fame motive in my study with that of other motives—say, the power motive or the money motive—if we had any facts, but we do not. It's not without interest, however, to see how the 2 percent estimate of the fame motive compares with the incidence of some well-known clinical illnesses among the noninstitutionalized U.S. population aged 18 and over: schizophrenia, 1 percent; bipolar disorder, 1.5 percent; and narcissistic personality disorder in nonclinical populations, 1.5 percent.[9]

Daydreams, Expectations, and Importance

In addition to the millions for whom fame is their primary desire, there are many millions more who think about fame and becoming famous. A number of national surveys have probed into how people relate to the idea of fame. They have asked such questions as "Do you daydream about fame?" "Do you expect ever to be famous?" and "Is it important to be famous—and would you like to be?"

Daydreams

In 1987, a national telephone sample of two thousand adults was questioned as follows: "Most people at some time or another daydream about what it would be like if they were famous. Have you ever daydreamed about being famous?" More than half (57 percent) of the respondents said yes. The same question was asked in two subsequent surveys. In 1993, 50 percent of respondents said yes, and in 1997, 52 percent said yes.[10]

Earlier, in 1984, another national survey posed the question more elaborately: "Most people spend at least a small part of their waking hours daydreaming and thinking about different things. Some of these daydreams may be complete flights of fancy, others just simple, like a hungry person thinking about lunch. Here is a list of some things people might be expected to daydream about from time to time." In addition to "being famous," the list included 21 possible choices, such as "being a great athlete," "being beautiful or handsome," and "being elected to political office." Of the 2,005 respondents, 17 percent said they do daydream about being famous. The identical question was asked in four other national surveys, one earlier in 1979 and the others in 1989, 1992, and 1997. The results were consistent across the two decades, ranging from 17 percent to 21 percent of respondents saying yes.[11]

Why is there such a difference between the percentage of yes responses in the first set of surveys (approximately 50 percent) and the percentage in the second set (18 percent)? The answer lies in the questions themselves. The first set of respondents was asked only if they daydream about becoming famous, limiting the question to that single subject and requiring only a yes or no answer. The second set asked respondents to disclose their favorite subject for daydreaming from a number of likely alternatives, including becoming famous. Instead of giving an easy answer, they had to make a thoughtful choice.

Although "becoming famous" was outranked by other daydreams in the second set of surveys, it might well have scored higher in all of the surveys were it not for the tendency among respondents in any survey on any subject to favor the most socially acceptable answer. American society in general looks askance at people who keep saying, "Look at me!" The assertion that "most people daydream," which all of the surveys began with, was an attempt to counteract that prejudice by reassuring respondents that their thoughts and views, whatever they might be, are widely shared and accepted.

Note that the findings of these surveys—eight of them, conducted over two decades—contradict the speculation in the United States that desire for fame is spreading, especially among young people. Collectively, they show no increase in the numbers who say they daydream about fame. While it's true that the Internet has opened a world of new opportunities for calls for attention, there is as yet no evidence that the fame motive itself significantly widened its scope.

Expectations

A national survey of a thousand adults conducted in 2000 had a sharper focus: "It has been said that eventually everyone will get their fifteen minutes of fame, that is, be well known or widely recognized for an accomplishment or activity for a short period of time. How likely do you think [it is that] this will really happen to you?" The respondents (aged 20 and older) were drawn from two hundred million noninstitutionalized adults in the United States. Thirty percent of them, representing sixty million people, said it was either very likely or somewhat likely that they would be famous for fifteen minutes. The survey did not report whether or to what degree they would welcome such an event.[12]

Importance

Three surveys of American adults conducted around 1990 found that about 30 percent would like to be famous.[13] One asked 1,011 adults, "Would you like to be famous, that is, popular, well known, or widely recognized for your accomplishments, activities, abilities, expertise, or opinions?" Thirty percent said yes.[14] A second survey asked 1,654 adults, "People have different ideas about what it means to be successful. I am going to read you a list. For each item, please tell me whether it is a very important element of your idea of success, a somewhat important element, or a relatively unimportant element." Eight percent of respondents considered "being prominent or famous" to be "very important," and 25 percent responded "somewhat important."[15] A third survey asked 1,205 adults, "I am going to read some conditions that you could possibly have in your life in the future. How desirable would it be for you to achieve fame or public recognition—very, somewhat, not too, not at all?" Ten percent of respondents said that fame was "very desirable," and 26 percent responded "somewhat desirable."[16] If we combine the "very" and "somewhat" responses in the second and third surveys, they come to about 33–36 percent and so are similar to the results of the first survey.

Two additional surveys asked about the desirability or importance of becoming famous but included no "somewhat" data. In one, 1,005 adults were asked the same question about achieving fame as in the third survey just mentioned. Ten percent said that it was "very desirable," and 90 percent responded "somewhat/not too/not at all desirable/don't know."[17] The other survey asked 1,296 adults, "Now, I'd like to talk with you about a term you are probably familiar with, The American Dream. People have different ideas about what the term 'The American Dream' means to them personally. I am going to read you a list. For each item, please tell me whether it is a very important element of your American Dream, a somewhat important element, or a relatively unimportant element." Five percent of respondents considered "being prominent or famous" to be "very important," and 95 percent responded "somewhat important/unimportant/don't know."[18] It seems likely—or at least a good guess—that in the two instances where "somewhat" data is lacking, it would have been close to the 25 percent reported by the preceding survey.

What can we conclude from these surveys? First, many people dream and think about fame (it costs nothing to do so), but the dreamers are not greatly motivated to become famous. They are content to dream about fame without imposing a reality check on their dreams and therefore feel no need to do anything to fulfill them. Second, when asked to make a choice among many possible real-life goals—money, career, sex, marriage, a happy family life, intelligence, courage, beauty—the number who say that fame is their primary objective over all the others shrinks to a small minority of about 2 percent. Even the lower figure, however, leads to my conservative estimate, cited at the beginning of this book, that four million adults in the United States are striving to become or remain famous.

Around the World

Currently, the United States is accused of being obsessed with fame. Here are some allegations.

The only life American society seems to value: celebrity.

Fame has become America's greatest export.

Today the gifted as well as the deranged among us are struggling to be famous—the way earlier Americans struggled to be saved.

People do everything with respect to that third eye, which is the eye of *People Magazine.*

Celebrity has a power over us almost as transcendent as our sexual or monetary desires.

In my view, however, that all societies include individuals who are motivated by fame, because all societies will include some people who are rejected by others and need to compensate for their lack of acceptance and approval. Therefore, I doubt that the fame motive is more widespread in the United States than in other societies. I think that its incidence would be much the same.

German and Beijing Surveys

To test my belief about the fame motive in other societies, I had two surveys made—one in Germany and one in Beijing—to generate findings comparable to those we have about the United States (see "German and Beijing Surveys" at the back of this book). My method was to examine existing fame-related surveys made in the United States for questions with two characteristics: they had to use telephone interviews, as in the United States; they also had to report their findings by gender, age, and education, so that I could compare the German, Beijing, and U.S. survey findings on those social categories (which I do in chapter 3).

Only two surveys met both requirements. One asked, "It has been said that eventually everyone will get their fifteen minutes of fame, that is, be well known or widely recognized for an accomplishment or activity for a short period of time. How likely do you think [it is that] this will really happen to you?" The other asked, "Most people at some time or another daydream about what it would be like if they were famous. Have you ever daydreamed about being famous?"

In reply to the first question, 48 percent of the German and 45 percent of the Beijing respondents said they thought it very likely or somewhat likely that they would get their fifteen minutes of fame—both considerably higher percentages than the U.S. figure of 31 percent. In reply to the second question, 31 percent of both the German and Beijing respondents said they had daydreamed about being famous. This compares to the U.S. figures of 52 percent and 57 percent (in different surveys).

The differences in the responses may well be caused by the somewhat different meanings that English expressions like "daydream" and "fifteen minutes of fame" can acquire in translation. In the German survey, the words *fame* and *famous* were translated by the words *beruehmt* and *bekannt.* In the Beijing survey, they were translated by the words *cheng ming* and *ming ren.* Both the German and Chinese words carry the meaning that fame is earned through notable and valued achievements, whereas the English words are not similarly restricted—one can be famous for almost anything. It also may be that the German and Beijing respondents viewed fame more idealistically, as something to be hoped for, than their U.S. equivalents (in the first question) and at the same time were less inclined than Americans to daydream about anything so distant (in the second question).

Despite these differences, I believe that the survey results confirm that the idea of fame and the fame motive are indeed part of very different cultures. In a recent study in Germany, a psychologist investigated "lifespan longing" (*sehnsucht*), defined as the desire and longing for alternative realizations of life. In this study, 299 persons aged 19 to 81 were asked to "generate their three most important lifespan longings [and] provide short descriptions." Of the 892 longings described by the respondents, 20 directly referred to fame: for example, "there were longings for becoming a recognized author, painter, or rock star, as well as for fame or recognition in general."[19] What's striking to me here is that 20 out of 892 is slightly over 2 percent, which matches the 2 percent in the American surveys who chose fame as their number one life goal.

Observations

As part of my research, I reviewed anthropological studies included in the major archives of cross-cultural data, such as the one at Yale University. I found no persuasive observations of differences in the fame motive from one society to another. Frequently, in fact, I noted similarities.

A 2003 article from the *Shanghai Star* reports,

> Our national enthusiasm about securing a niche in the much revered *Guinness Book of Records* has not abated with the passage of time.
>
> On the contrary, it is gaining momentum every day, although the motivation behind all our frenzied attempts at doing the impossible is controversial.
>
> Our perseverance and pioneering spirit in blazing a trail nobody has ever trodden before is no doubt admirable. In order to achieve a world record and generate a stunning effect, we defy great risks, even hazarding our lives. We place a large wager on what we pledge to accomplish, inasmuch as our fortune is closely linked to its success or failure.
>
> But, generally speaking, commercialism has a big role to play in all this ballyhoo. In all likelihood, we may become overnight celebrities thanks to the media hype, even if we were foiled in our daring plans.
>
> In a word, we look upon it as a short cut to fame and wealth.[20]

A Web survey in Karachi elicited answers to the question "What do you tend to daydream about?" Some Muslim men and women in their twenties (speaking Urdu and Punjabi) said, "Being famous." Writing of an incident in Sri Lanka, on the Unawatuna beach on the southwest coast, Oliver Standing, in an essay entitled "Barefoot on the Golden Silvery Sands," reports, "One endearing character tried to sell me some puppets. He wasn't at all put out when I turned down his offer, merely pulling out a battered German guidebook with a happy cry of 'I am world famous.' He had a full-page color photo and a mile-wide grin."[21]

It's often said by scholars that a striking difference between the United States and Japan is that fame is unimportant in Japan—that the Japanese wish is to "line up side by side," neither ahead of nor behind one another, rather than stand out. Within Japanese culture, it is in social relationships, obligations, and duties that one derives a sense of security; the individual's goal is to function smoothly within a large encompassing collective. Nevertheless, Japan has its famous golfers and baseball players and its eleven- and thirteen-year-old rock stars. Material on a Japanese Web site suggests that indifference to fame is far from universal. The pages were written by the students of Kyoto Sangyo University for non-Japanese who would like to learn about famous people in modern-day Japan. They list a wide assortment of famous Japanese, male and female, in such categories as musicians, politicians, television and movie personalities, writers, and so on.

The Japanese language is also not inattentive to fame, as the following variety of descriptive vocabulary demonstrates:

becoming famous	*jinkounikaisha*
famous	*nadakai*
infamous	*akumyoutakai, akumyyoudakai*
to become famous	*yonitatsu, yonideru*
to become famous overnight	*suiseinoyouniarawareru*
fame	*hyouban, meisei, yuumei, eimei, imei, reibun*
military fame	*bumei*
to burst into fame	*suiseinoyouniarawareru*
to win fame	*namaewohaseru*
desire for fame	*meiyoshin*

Other linguistic evidence supports my conviction that interest in fame and the fame motive itself are worldwide. A search through some twenty language dictionaries, from Albanian to Yiddish, reveals that every language has words meaning "fame" or "famous" or "fame motive" (see "Fame in Different Languages"). (I have been cautioned that these words, when translated, may sometimes wander from their English meanings, but rather than try to sort through the opinions of many different linguists, I've accepted the dictionary definitions.)

Proof that fame and those who strive for it attract and may even inspire an international audience is demonstrated both in and by the *Guinness Book of Records* (lately, the *Guinness World Records 2000*).[22] This well-known compendium (which includes "only those records which improve upon previous records or which are newly significant in having become the subject of widespread and preferably international competitiveness") sold nearly two million copies in the first nine months of 2000. The annual series started in 1960 and has become the world's largest-selling copyrighted book. In recent years, it has been published in twenty-six languages, including Arabic, Hebrew, and Slovenian. The sixty-seven countries where it is regularly sold range from Algeria to Zimbabwe. All of this suggests that fame is a universal fascination. (See *"Guinness Book of Records."*)

Ignorance, Denial, and Repression

Survey results can be illuminating but also misleading. When respondents are asked, "Do you prefer chocolate ice cream or vanilla?" we can rely on their answers. Their attitudes toward fame are harder to pin down; statements made in a personal interview may clash with a subject's behavior as reported by others.

Other research methods—personal interviews, observations of behavior—might show different results. Self-descriptions in surveys of one's "inner state" are not the only way to measure the existence of the fame motive. There are other kinds of descriptions (though no personality tests). There are descriptions of a person by others. There are goal-directed actions and other behaviors that are indicative of a motivational state.

Whatever the source of our information, I believe that it underestimates the strength of the fame motive. In my experience, in observing and listening to people and in conversations about fame, I found that several of my friends motivated by fame—people whom I knew either wanted to become famous (sometimes with a passion) or, if already famous, wanted to become more so—would declare vigorously that they had no interest in fame. Even though they carefully followed the careers of contemporaries who kept trying to be famous, they never acknowledged that they might be doing the same.

There are three reasons why people may underreport their motivation for fame. First is ignorance about our own desires.[23] There are often times in life when we do not know the reasons for our actions. If someone asks, "Why are you doing that?" we may give a reason, but it is likely to be the wrong one. Sometimes you might even say, "I wish I didn't behave this way," but you do not know why you do. In chapter 1, I wrote as if everyone motivated by fame has a self-image of themselves as famous, in the present or future. However, some may desire fame and pursue it but not know in their minds that this is their motive. For such people, the goal of fame is never imagined.

The second reason is denial. A belief about the morality of wanting to be famous exists in every culture. In some the motive for fame may be rewarded and elaborated; in others it may be suppressed and punished. In chapter 3 I describe how in the United States its value varies by occupation: less within the legal profession, for example, than by the show business. Why these differences? Is the fame motive shameful? Is it taboo, like talking about wanting a lot of sex, or simply socially unacceptable to state that one wants to be famous? It certainly is viewed differently than the desire to be wealthy, which is openly admitted to both self and others.

Although I have no information about how American adults feel about this—about whether it is wrong to talk about wanting to be famous—I believe that most would say it is unacceptable behavior. A friend observed, "I'm sure that a lot of people feel that wanting fame is a bit immodest." Another said, "I think people hide their desire for fame because they find it a rather shabby motive that they don't want to be associated with. They want to pretend they really don't care about that—they just pretend they want to do something splendid but they don't care whether they're famous or not." Yet another friend explained, "I think that some people don't want to deal with the nakedness of the fame motive—they want to dress up a really selfish motive—by saying, 'I'm doing good in the world,' for instance. I mean there are many ways to cloak the fame motive that seem honorable and allow you to live with yourself."

The third reason is repression. Repression, as we know, is to force ideas and impulses that are painful to the conscious mind—thoughts that arouse fear, for example—into the unconscious, where they can be concealed and kept from being known to us. Can the fame motive be unconscious? Of course. If the social norms are strong and the social control intense, so that we—either as child or adult—have been severely punished for expressing a wish for fame, the wish may become buried, causing us to deny to ourselves that this unacceptable desire exists within us. A friend observed, "There is a little, dirty motive at the center." Furthermore, the experiences of rejection and disapproval can be equally punishing to recall and also likely to be repressed. Thus the fame motive and the experiences that gave rise to it are buried together.

Summary

- In addition to the four million persons in the United States who have fame as their most important life goal, there is a much larger number who dream about becoming famous.
- The fame motive exists in some degree in all societies around the world.
- There is an unknown but substantial number of people with the fame motive who deny it to the world and keep it a secret even to themselves.

3 ☆ Differences among Us in Desire for Fame

Passion, Indifference, and Aversion

In their measurements of motives for power, sex, money, and other goals, psychologists use questionnaires, interviews, direct observations, experimental arousal, ranking and rating scales, projective tests, content analysis, and forced choices. They haven't yet created tests to measure the desire for fame; a search through the handbooks of personality measurement turns up nothing of value. To be sure, such entries as "enjoys being center of attention" or "desires recognition" appear occasionally in measures of other personality characteristics, but nowhere are they brought together as a measure of fame. Hence I rely on my own research.

A *Barbara Walters Special* television program included interviews with perhaps thirty men and women in show business on how they handle their fame and their interest in being famous. Arnold Schwarzenegger said, "It's what I wanted, I enjoy it." Alan Alda expressed indifference: "You do it for a small group of friends—if you are famous in the larger world, so be it."[1] Naturally, individuals will differ in their attitudes toward fame and the fame motive. Some will want to be famous. Others—most of us—will be more or less indifferent. Still others, a few, will both reject the fame motive for themselves and disapprove of it in others.

Passion

The motivation to become famous ranges from strong to weak. At the strong end, it is a powerful passion. At the weak end, it blends into indifference. An observer who describes this passion as a "hunger for recognition—to know that strangers recognize your name, to watch them startle and stare when you walk into the room," says, "That's what fame is, the recognition of strangers. *Have they noticed me yet?*"[2]

In an interview, one man reported on another, "I think he is someone who wants to be as famous as Freud. He even said so on one occasion. Whether he was having fun or just very serious, I'm not sure, but someone who says something like that is clearly driven by fame." Another interviewee said,

> The people I have known who are really obsessed with fame at the same time display qualities of character which are very difficult to tolerate. Now it just may be that I've been exposed to a strange sample of people, but the ones who really stand out in my mind are people who are, I mean, they are just driven to go on to the next great project and the next great project after that. My wife has a wonderful phrase for characterizing what I'm trying to get at. Such a person is someone who can take any topic, any topic, and go, as she puts it, "from zero to me" in an instant. They have a way of featuring themselves in interpersonal conversations. If you were calling such a person and asked the question you're asking me, their answer would be, "Well, that's a subject I haven't written on."

Robert Gottlieb described how Tallulah Bankhead decided as a teenager to be an actress and had an overwhelming desire to be famous or even infamous. The singer Christina Aguilera said, "When I see all of these people screaming and chanting and holding these signs that they made just for me . . . I feel like I'm floating on air. It's the most incredible feeling, and I've always wanted it."[3]

In her article "Death on the CNN Curve," Lisa Belkin describes a fireman's sudden and unexpected elevation to fame.[4] In a headlined event in Midland, Texas, Robert O'Donnell saved a little girl's life. She had fallen down a pipe, and O'Donnell, one among many who helped in her rescue, happened to be the one who struggled through a tunnel to bring her out—to on-site live coverage by the TV networks. For O'Donnell, there were many consequences: a blizzard of fan letters, a made-for-TV movie, and much else—all of which he seems to have relished.

O'Donnell's fame was probably unintended. When he was inching through the tunnel to save little Jessica, he probably was thinking of her, not himself. Or did he also have an image of himself as the rescuer who now would be famous? Had the fame motive shown itself in O'Donnell before he became famous? Perhaps it was hidden. It turned out, though, that he very much wanted the fame that came to him. In the years that followed, he sought to maintain and even increase his fame. In the end, eight years later, he committed suicide.

Indifference

In my research, I've come across many people who evidently had never thought much about fame. During one brief conversation in which I mentioned my interest in the fame motive, the man I was interviewing stared at me blankly, as if nothing had been said. The idea of people wanting to become famous was new to him—simply not part of his thinking. "I don't know anyone who wants to be famous," he said. "I can't imagine a day when I don't play golf. How is fame different from winning?" When asked for her views about fame and famous people, another interviewee declared, "I've never thought about it." When asked if she knew of anyone who wanted to be famous, she came up with Donald Trump. A friend said, "I was lucky. I learned early in life that I don't have to be famous to be happy. I concluded that trying to be famous is goofy—putting your head on all those coins—and that I don't have to be famous to have a good life."

In one of the two surveys in the United States that report the most positive reactions to thinking about fame, 50 percent of the respondents said they had never dreamed about fame. In the other survey, which asked, "Would you like to be famous, that is, popular, well known, or widely recognized for your accomplishments, activities, abilities, expertise, or opinions?" 69 percent answered no.[5] Although the U.S. population mostly consists of people who are indifferent to fame, there undoubtedly are some who have a "feigned indifference," denying an interest that really exists. For the multitude, however, I'm convinced that the indifference is genuine.

In an interview, a woman psychologist said,

> I don't think about fame. But if I had, let me tell you, I guess it could have been my ten or fifteen minutes of fame when you gave me the opportunity to be on the *Today Show* . . . That would be the closest . . . People e-mailing me, "I saw you on the *Today Show*." Kids I went to high school with. That was my fame experience. I've had a few others,

you know—when I got an award and stuff like that. But it's not something I would seek out. I would do it, but I would not want to seek it out, because I didn't enjoy it that much, to be honest with you. I was glad after it was over. I think I enjoy privacy and just doing smaller things for people here.

Well, and they gave me the chance to—a lot of people said, "Well, why didn't you go to New York?" They told me to come down—they'd get me a limousine, they'd pick me up at the airport—and I said I don't think it's worth it to get on national television for fifteen minutes for me to travel to New York, leave my family, all this kind of stuff. There was other stuff I needed to do that day. Is there a fame motive here?

In another interview, a woman talked about her early career.

I want to say one thing here that kind of brought very clearly to mind in the relatively early stages of my career that I was not fueled by the pursuit of fame in any way, shape, or form. Shortly after I came, I gave a talk at a brown-bag lunch, and it was about links between personality and social structure. This is a very strong experimentally oriented social psych program here, and you know social structure is just not part of what they've studied, so I was basically espousing the things we always espouse about working on these disciplinary boundaries. And afterwards, [___], probably the best-known social psychologist here—came up to me and said, "Why are you studying this? You're never going to be famous for this kind of work."

He did?

He said that to me, and I just flat out said to him, "You know, I'm not interested in being famous." I mean, it was just an immediate response. I'm not. You know. I do what I do, I study what I study, because it's interesting to me and strikes me as important. I could not care less whether or not, you know, this is on some trajectory to fame.

What happened?

I think he was shocked. I think he was absolutely shocked, because I think his assumption was, you know, you want to study things that are going to bring you a lot of visibility and acclaim, and this is not one of them.

I mean he just kind of brought into high relief and just basically said, "You know, aren't you going after this?" and I'd never really given it much thought before. And so it just became—because I was questioned about it—just became immediately clear to me that that's not a motive I have!

I certainly have an achievement ethic, given the distance I've traveled from the world I started from. My achievement motives have been extreme in many ways, but I think I have insight into what has fueled that, and it was from the beginning a deep sense of needing to compensate, needing to compensate for a family who—even in my little town, there were clearly gradations of social hierarchy, and, you know, my friends, most of my friends, had families who were in a different level than my family. Things like being embarrassed to invite my friends for a sleepover because our house wasn't very nice, and, you know, the kind of cars that people drive, and being in a family that never took a vacation. Added to that, what in some way is probably the most pivotal early experience in my life was having an older sister who became pregnant at the end of her senior year in high school, and she went away to a home for unwed mothers because, you know, this was a time in which good Christian people didn't talk about abortion or certainly would never take action on that. So in a small town like that, everyone knew, and it was this huge shameful experience.

And so what became my quest—I mean, I didn't grasp it fully at the time—but my quest was basically to regain my family's pride. And it was powerful. It was powerful. I wanted my parents to feel so proud of me that they could forget about all of this other agony that they'd gone through. Now it wasn't about being famous. It could easily have looked like a pursuit for kind of my own glory and recognition, but it was about reestablishing my family's respect and pride.

Aversion

A firm indifference to fame may be close to aversion. Some of us who are famous become so averse to fame that we reject it absolutely, like the reclusive author J. D. Salinger. I see several reasons for aversion to fame.

First, fame may bring danger. Probably a thousand persons in New York City worth more than a hundred million dollars apiece remain unknown except to a few. Many on *Fortune* magazine's list of the five hundred wealthiest people are not well known. Perhaps the achievements that brought them wealth are of little interest to society or the media, but it's more likely that many on the *Fortune* list value their privacy and choose to remain obscure.

Anonymous philanthropy provides many examples of this choice. A friend told me, "Recently I saw in the newspaper that a huge donation was given to some of the Jewish day schools in the Boston area, and it was from multiple families that were anonymous, and as I looked at that, I thought, this is great that people want to do good things and help but don't want anyone to know who they are." The friend observed that the donors' anonymity may be religious in character, inspired by Maimonides' famous statement on the Eight Levels of Charity, in which the philosopher says it is best that the recipient of charity not know who his or her benefactor is.

Many philanthropic gifts come unencumbered by the name of the donor. Andrew W. Mellon and his son Paul, huge benefactors of the National Gallery of Art, insisted on keeping their names off the building. Priscilla Bullitt Collins of Seattle, who has given tens of millions of dollars to the city, reportedly said, "I'm different . . . I don't want my name on anything. There is nothing—and there had better not be." Cornell University reported that an anonymous donor had pledged one hundred million dollars to help revamp undergraduate housing. (A year earlier, Sanford and Joan Weill had given the same amount to support Cornell's medical school, which was renamed the Weill Medical College.)

Of course, one can't always be sure whether anonymous philanthropy expresses humility or simply a wish to avoid the attentions that fame can attract. The author James Michener became famous through *Tales of the South Pacific*. That and other books brought him great wealth—more than one hundred million dollars—which he gave away during his lifetime "anonymously to escape requests." He couldn't avoid fame for his achievements as an author but shunned it as a philanthropist—though less out of humility than self-protection, for his gifts were not to remain anonymous in perpetuity. While Michener's beneficiaries were required to keep his name in confidence during his lifetime, they could reveal it after his death—as many did.

Let me note here a special subclass of fame aversion, in which a person who desires to be famous and whose deeds are extraordinary and widely known avoids being identified by name because the achievements are so deviant, mainly illegal, that they would bring on infamy (rather than fame) and perhaps punishment as well. Criminals are obvious examples, but even they may in time succumb to the fame motive. A study of check forgers reports, "To be successful at forging checks it is essential never to take anyone into one's confidence. This means that you can't let anyone know how good you are at what you do. In the end, this proves to be utterly untenable and most systematic check forgers become knowingly careless and commit acts which almost guarantee that they will be caught. When they are, they then confess to what they have been doing in hopes that law enforcement personnel will appreciate how skillful they have been."[6]

Another reason for avoiding fame is the destructive effect it can have on one's work. Leo Braudy, the brilliant historian of fame, states, in *The Frenzy of Renown*, that English poets and authors of the nineteenth century were "caught in the conflicting pressures of an unprecedented fame culture."[7] He ascribes the strong aversion to public fame that many of them shared to a conviction that being famous stifled and degraded true effort. (Charles Dickens, arguably the greatest of them, had an opposite view; he relished public attention and traded on his fame as a novelist to become a huge success giving paid public readings from his works. Like so many fame seekers, he was the victim of a deprived childhood.) A woman with a family who has devoted herself to international good works and caring for others explained in an interview how fame intruded on and impeded her work.

I have two circles now. One is in my community, and now I have gotten a reputation for my teaching, and people who I don't know are calling me and asking me to teach their children—children who were born long after I began to teach. And that's been interesting for two reasons. One is, well, isn't this nice, because I can continue to be useful, and the other is, you know, it does feel nice to have some kind of feedback for the work I did. Now in the other circle, I find it to be really not. This is in the spiritual and religious education I had been doing for our whole network around the world. I did the work because it needed to be done and they really wanted me to do it, but what I hadn't expected was that people were now going to start approaching me with requests and invitations and activities.

In this you are internationally famous, aren't you?

Yes, and I find that to get in the way. It makes me self-conscious. This is a conflict. Because the work was what was important to me, and I wanted to get it done and anonymously. It gave me a lot of freedom.

There was no self-consciousness involved. It was almost, I feel it needs to be done, I know I can do this, and I want to do it, but then, when people start looking for me as an individual, suddenly—I can't put it to words—but I have to do this anonymously. I don't like it. It doesn't enhance my work. It's just that I'm the one who's happening to do the work and make it happen. I feel good about that—but I really don't really want people looking for me.

You wish you'd stayed anonymous?

I would have preferred to.

Another kind of aversion to fame occurs when people who want fame become famous for the wrong reason. Instead of achieving the fame they desire, they become famous for something of little interest or value to them or even for something they dislike. Saul Steinberg, a well-known artist, is most famous for his poster "View of the World from 9th Avenue." Originally a cover for the *New Yorker,* it is one of the most popular posters ever, with many unauthorized imitations and printings. Steinberg reportedly was angry about the damage to his reputation from this notoriety. "I am a most discreet man," he said. "I have refused to be photographed. I rarely grant interviews. I want to be left alone. My dream has been to have a quiet [recognition] among my artist colleagues. Now this whole episode has made me comical. It has reduced me to 'the man who did that poster.'"

Scientists whose work receives media coverage sometimes are angry because they believe they have done or can do much better work than what is being publicized. Harriet Zuckerman, a sociologist who studied Nobel Prize recipients, summarized what these extraordinary achievers said when asked about the scientific work for which they were honored: "Nearly half of the laureates who were interviewed, while conceding the scientific significance of their research, were convinced that it was not their best work."[8]

Famous for achievements he thought little of and angry at the fame that he received was the painter Mark Rothko. He is reported to have said, "Buried in fame—but for work I knew to be absolutely worthless! This was my sentence: I must endure 30 years of being called distinguished by people incapable of telling good works from inferior." In the end, he took his own life.

Still another cause of aversion to fame is found among people who have been taught that a desire to become famous is wrong—a bad and selfish motive—and to place high value on humility and modesty and obscurity. On a woman's fiftieth birthday, one of her daughters paid to have a childhood picture of her mother appear in the local newspaper. No name was attached, but some people recognized the woman, whose looks had changed little over the years. The woman was upset by the attention and reacted angrily, telling her daughter, "I'm taking you out of my will." Believing it was wrong, she truly did not want to "be famous" and was contemptuous of people who did. A woman scholar reported similar feelings in an interview.

> I've now reached a point in my own career in which there is some recognition. I mean, it's not high-flying fame, but it's certainly far more recognition than I ever expected would be part of my life. And getting this award—if you can believe it, my most significant emotion about getting that award was embarrassment. I did not enjoy it. I don't want to stand up and talk about myself. I kept digging into it and asking myself, "Why do I find this recognition of my work so discomforting?" And I realized that for me there is an abiding awareness that fame and acclaim and doing well in life breeds resentment in lots of other people, and I don't want to deal with that. I don't want to deal with other people's jealousy, other people's resentment, because I think, when you get to that kind of upper level of high-achieving people, that what you see there is an enormous amount of competition. I think it's evil and sick, and I would just rather stay out of the limelight. I don't want to be there. It's not gratifying to me; it's embarrassing.
>
> *That is very interesting. I think of you as being famous.*
>
> Yeah, well, I don't want to be.

A case of what might be called reverse aversion occurs among people who have the fame motive but wish they didn't. As I said in chapter 2, they may be ashamed of being motivated by a craving that, to them, is so unworthy, even evil, that they try to put it aside and even deny its existence. As a reaction, they then may unconsciously adopt the opposite of their true, but repressed, feelings—like a man with homosexual leanings who condemns homosexuality. To want something while wishing it would go away is a familiar human condition—like wanting a lover one would like to be rid of. When a person fears or despises fame yet still desires it, aversion may follow.

Socialization and Social Roles

The social controls over how and when the fame motive may be expressed have two components: (1) one's inner views of how one should feel about the fame motive and when it is proper to acknowledge it and (2) the social pressure from others to follow the norms and rules that apply to one's station in life.[9]

Socialization

Society must shape the raw material of individual biology into persons suitable for the activities and requirements that society values. The word *socialization* refers to a process of learning through which we are prepared, with varying degrees of success, to meet the standards laid down by other members of society for our behavior in a variety of situations. These standards are attached to one or another of society's recognized roles, such as husband or wife, daughter or son, student, employee or boss, or simply citizen. Socialization is a continuous process, lasting throughout life. The new student, the army recruit, the young honeymooners—all are continuously socialized as, with age, they move into new stages of life. Through socialization, we acquire the knowledge, skills, and dispositions that make us more or less able members of society and learn the habits, beliefs, attitudes, and motives of our particular society and its subgroups, all so that we may perform satisfactorily in our expected roles.

In the end, every human motive must submit to the control of society. This includes sex, from flirting to rape; power and equality; money and dishonesty; even hunger and what, when, and where one eats. Socialization shapes our relationship to the biblical seven deadly sins—pride, anger, envy, greed, gluttony, lust, and sloth. So it may be with the fame motive, as, through contact with others, we are taught how to feel about it (whether it is good or bad) and how and when to express it or conceal it.

In what ways, if at all, do we educate our children about the fame motive? Many studies of child development describe how parents and society in general socialize children about aggression, achievement, sex, money, and so on. There seem to be no socialization studies about fame. While it's clear to parents and society that children will need to manage aggression, money, and sex, perhaps it seems much less likely that the fame motive will develop in and need to be managed by the average child. Hence there are no books for parents, magazine articles, or discussion groups about how a child should deal with it. For parents and children alike, there is plenty of available sex education but no such thing as fame education.

Although American culture is full of images of famous people, past and present, it largely ignores the fame motive itself. As individuals, we tend to learn about it on our own, from various and often conflicting sources of information. So those who grow up with the fame motive in their makeup have no rules to consult on how to manage it or what to do if they happen to become famous.

What socialization there is seems mostly disapproving of the desire for fame. A mother says, "I was brought up not to be noticed. My mother taught me that being a good mother was the correct way to live." A seven-year-old girl diving into a swimming pool at a resort hotel may call to the crowd around the pool, "Doesn't anybody want to watch me?" She hasn't yet been socialized into controlling herself and her demand for attention. Later, her parents might say, "Don't be a show-off" and "Don't call attention to yourself" or might even quote the proverb "Fools' names and fools' faces oft appear in public places."

In an interview, a man described what he learned about fame in his childhood.

> In the environment that many of us grew up in, fame was almost viewed as a negative.
>
> *How?*
>
> Well, I could talk about my father, who was a famous man in his own right. He was a neurosurgeon—I can remember how we traveled both abroad and in this country to medical meetings where my father spoke and received, you know, a lot of honors. But he was the most humble man in the world, and fame was almost a negative as far as he was concerned. He wanted to be known for what he did for his fellow man, and being in the headlines didn't feature in that ambition.

In two more interviews, women told of their understanding about fame as children. One woman said,

> I remember, you don't want to draw attention to yourself. That was more the way I was raised. I don't know if we talked about it, but I saw the way my parents behaved was not to brag about things, not to put yourself out there, to be kind of humble and modest and not to kind of

flaunt things, including yourself. Not that we talked about it directly, but I learned that by modeling. And it's interesting because [my husband] is even more like that than I am, and so my kids are like that as well.

The other woman discussed fame more directly.

Certainly in the world that I grew up in, which would be, you know, rural working-class America, the pursuit of fame is not a virtue. I think it's in such strong opposition to things that are considered virtues, like humility and having a concern for others—that in many ways fame pursuits are in such stark contrast that it's almost, like, as a child you wouldn't need the instruction.

Were those values in your family?

Absolutely. I think they would have been mortified if I had ever said I hope to be famous.

Really?

Just mortified. Because it would have, to them, I think, conveyed an orientation to life that I'm in it just for myself, I'm in it for the glory, I'm not going after things that are valued and honored in their world.

Was there a religious factor in this?

I think so.

And what was that? What denomination, you might say?

Well, I grew up in what was called the First Christian Church, and it's not Pentecostal, but it was certainly kind of fundamentalist Christianity. In those kinds of religious orientations, we are viewed as sinners, so the best you could be hoping for would be to achieve some close communion with God and find your way to grace—but certainly not find your way to fame.

Social Roles

The customs we have for talking about a desire for fame—and especially about directly expressing a hope to become famous—vary from one community to another, from family to family, and especially among occupational roles in society. There are some sectors of endeavor that people who want to be famous will be sure to avoid—such as law or medicine or science, all of which traditionally have a low regard for fame seekers. Much the same applies in academic culture.

Cullen Murphy describes how academia censures "glory hounds," those who seek public fame apart from their academic status. She notes that academics are expected to lead an obscure life and that so many do so that in a recent poll, the number of respondents with no opinion about college teachers had doubled in the course of a year. According to the poll, people were not thinking about college teachers as often as they were not thinking about undertakers.[10] An example of how social constraints and the pursuit of fame can collide within the world of science is the career of the astrophysicist Carl Sagan: "More than half a billion viewers saw his own 13-episode television series, *Cosmos* . . . Sagan played the role of a star. He appeared on the *Tonight* show with Johnny Carson 26 times . . . He loved attention."[11] One interviewee explained the relationship between academics and fame further.

> For some reason, social scientists are embarrassed to talk about fame. It's like revealing a family secret. I don't understand why; they won't talk about sex, and they won't talk about fame. Machiavelli talked about it. Homer talked about it. So how come all these wise people talked about fame and now American social scientists don't? That's really very funny.
>
> *When we talked before, just briefly, you said something that has stuck with me. I think you said, "In a thousand seminars over the past decade and a half, the subject has never come up at [a major research center]." I was dumbfounded by that, so I thought I'd ask why?*
>
> Well, I'm not sure I can answer why, but it still hasn't come up since I said that.
>
> *I'm wondering, how come there isn't a vocabulary here, how come there isn't any literature?*
>
> I think, I would say, that I am increasingly struck by the silence I observe in the social and behavioral sciences . . . Well, hold on a minute. Okay. Now I'm thinking of somebody who I encountered who absolutely does want to be famous; he wants to win the Nobel Prize in economics. He doesn't make any bones about this. I've been regaled

with stories from his colleagues about this, because every time some personal misfortune befalls him—a family crisis or whatever—he'll send an e-mail to his colleagues telling them that this has happened and he fears this will cost him the Nobel Prize.

And what's their reaction?

That they think he is a total complete outlier. I mean, he's an economist, for God's sake, and when you're an outlier among economists, that's really an accomplishment. But they just treat him as a completely alien human being. He's a complete pariah for this reason.

What's wrong with what he's saying?

Well, I think this is the way I would put it: that in a field like economics, the Nobel Prize is seen as a reward given to you by a community of people for accomplishments you have which were not motivated by the desire to win the prize but, rather, by the desire to advance basic knowledge of your field. So I think this is what is off-putting to people—you know, like Hollywood starlets and so on talking about wanting to be famous. It is a quality conferred on you by an audience of people and not something that you yourself voraciously claim.

As times change, the constraints on expressing the fame motive can also change. Patricia Fara writes about scientists of the later seventeenth and early eighteenth centuries, especially Isaac Newton, who sought public recognition in ways that would be scorned by his peers today. She describes how Newton paid for many portraits and busts to be put on display and how he sent out pictures of himself to reach a larger audience.[12] In the United States today, there seems to be a trend toward less constraint. A university professor commented on this in an interview.

Universities are starting to pay attention to fame with the stars that get recruited. You know, big money. There was a big story a couple years ago in the newspaper when Jane Fonda wanted to give money to Harvard for a center on gender and society and then the professor she wanted to direct it wound up getting wooed away by New York University. In the *New York Times,* there have been a few articles over the last year about these stars . . . Harvard is trying to steal people away from MIT and so on and so forth.

Trying to steal famous people.

I think an answer, in response to what you were saying about it's not as well accepted in academia—is that even universities, with the competition, are now starting to play into these academic stars, whether they are winning Nobel Prizes or Pulitzers or whatever it is, and that universities are looking at that as star quality, and they're famous and the universities want that. I think fame is now entering into academia as well, and the "prize" professors as they call them.

Careers in show business offer sharp contrasts to the lives of scientists. Films, TV, theater, and music are all approved places to hunt for fame. The movie *Fame* reported on the lives of students attending the Fiorella H. LaGuardia High School of Music and Art and the Performing Arts in New York City. Applicants to the school come from each of the city's five boroughs, from the city's diverse ethnic and cultural mix, and from every walk of life. Of the more than fifteen thousand who apply each year, less than 5 percent are admitted. It was the first school of its kind; there are now performing arts schools like it in all major U.S. cities. The TV series *Fame* that followed the movie in 1982–83 dealt with the hopes and ambitions of a group of students aspiring to careers in show business. A musical comedy-drama also followed the film, centering on a group of young students (actors, dancers, and musicians) through the four-year period of 1980–84.

One interviewee said, "Nobody cares about fame—only those kooks who go to Hollywood to try to be famous." But there is evidence all around us that the speaker was mistaken. We have the television show *American Idol,* on which the judges say that the contestants are obsessed with fame. We have the British television show *Pop Idol,* in which the candidates universally declare that they applied because "I want to be famous." Fame is their prime objective, not a career in singing.

At the other end of the spectrum, lawyers, doctors, and businessmen rarely speak of wanting to become famous. Said one, "If you go into business, you give up thinking about fame." Said another, "It just never occurred to me. I never thought about the word, never thought about famous people." Authors seem to fall between these two extremes. They may choose to live quiet lives (as have Barbara Tuchman and John Hersey) or to seek fame (as have Ernest Hemingway, William Buckley, and Norman Mailer). In a *New Yorker* cartoon, as a couple arrive at a cocktail party, the woman tells her companion to relax, that he's a famous author and people expect him to talk about himself.

Research on occupational choice shows that most of us end up in an occupation that fits our talent and interest. For some, this works out easily: those with a fame motive go into show business; those without it go into conventional business. For others, people who commit to an occupation that conflicts with their attitude toward fame, the fit can be awkward. A woman says of her son, "I don't know that he wants to be famous, but to be famous would be part of his success. I'm sure he wants to be successful, and being successful in the music business, the performing music business, would involve being famous. How can he sort it out in his head? I imagine it's a little difficult to do if you're a performer and your career rests actually on your being well known." When success in one's career inevitably brings fame—as with pop singers, champion athletes, and so on—being recognized on the street, whether welcome or not, simply goes with the job. The tennis star Lindsay Davenport is reported to have said, "I love playing tennis, I love going out there and competing. I don't enjoy having a lot of attention. I get a little uncomfortable with that. When I quit tennis, I hope it kind of goes away, back into anonymity."

Consider the following four different relationships between the fame motive and occupational norms:

1. A person wants to be famous and goes into show business or becomes a successful author. The motive and the role are in harmony.

2. A person does not want to be famous but goes into sports, movies, or politics, where the fame motive is assumed and where success is rewarded with fame. The motive and the role are at odds.

3. A person wants to be famous but is in an occupation where the motive is censured, such as wanting to be a famous professor, scientist, or businessman. Again, the motive and the role are at odds.

4. A person doesn't care about fame and ends up in an occupation where fame is not part of the culture, such as the law, the clergy, school teaching, and so on. There is harmony between the fame motive (or rather, its absence) and the occupational norm.

The last category, fortunately, is where most of us end up. But what happens to the people in the second and third categories? Do they exchange one occupation for another? Do they slog on in frustration? Must they pretend to be interested in fame when they're not? Must they subdue their motive for fame and seek it outside their occupations or keep changing careers in pursuit of an occupation receptive to the pursuit of fame?

Society has established some general guidelines for dealing with the fame motive. While no jail sentence is imposed for ostentatious attention seeking or self-promotion, there well may be censure for such comments as "We don't talk about that here" or "We don't do that kind of thing" and, most of all, the silent censure of frowns, pursed lips, heavy sighs, and other body language conveying disapproval, perhaps leading to ostracism in extreme cases. Reactions like those are mild compared to the civil complaints and lawsuits employed by society to control other kinds of disapproved behavior, such as hate language, unwanted sexual advances, and the invasion of property rights. Nevertheless, to a person motivated by fame, censures like those I've cited can be extremely demoralizing.

Our Gender, Age, and Education

The surveys in the United States, Germany, and Beijing described in chapter 2 questioned men and women, older and younger people, and people of different levels of education on their daydreams and expectations about fame (but not about fame as their primary motive). (See "Gender, Age, and Education Differences.") To sum up the findings in all three survey locations, the incidence of dreaming about being famous and expecting to become famous is somewhat greater for younger, well-educated men and is least for older, less-educated women. Humans are realistic in adjusting their dreams to the realities they experience in their lives—whether they're women or poorly educated or have reached old age. Dreams may be set aside or become less grand.

Gender

It is not true to say that women do not think about fame. Although the surveys show that more men than women say they daydream about fame and say they will get their fifteen minutes of fame, the differences, though statistically significant, are not large. From 5–10 percent more men than women say yes to the survey questions. There are more differences among females themselves and among men themselves than there are between men and women. These differences are consistent across the three societies and across almost five decades.

I see three possible explanations of these slight gender differences. First, there may be differences in the biogenetically based "need to belong" and/or differences in experiencing rejection and lack of approval that results in differences in the desire for fame. I find this hard to believe.

A second explanation lies in society's view of gender roles, that men strive for eminence and mastery while women seek affiliation, cooperation, and harmony with others. The poet Tennyson wrote, "Man dreams of fame while woman wakes to love."[13] But without any facts, should we assume a meaningful difference in how boys and girls are taught to feel about the fame motive and whether it's wrong to express it? That, too, seems doubtful.

A third possible source of the differences—the one I think most likely—is that women, more often than men, find themselves in roles where becoming famous is not feasible and where a desire for fame is viewed as inappropriate. The "Mother of the Year" award notwithstanding, the maternal role is not an avenue to fame. As one woman said, "Housewives never get out, so no one knows who you are or what you do." We might imagine a culture in which intimacy and affiliation are held to be of the highest importance and a source of fame to those who excel in those qualities, while holding down a paying job is viewed as unimportant, a mere existential necessity in which even excellence is undeserving of recognition and fame. But as we know, that's the opposite of how the world works, which perhaps is why, as a friend shrewdly observes, women often displace the desire for fame from self to a promising child.

Age

In the United States, because the mass media provide many opportunities for fame seekers to find an audience of strangers, one might suppose that the number of young people who dream of becoming famous is a rising tide over time. On the contrary, as noted earlier, national polls in the United States dating from 1970 to 1997 and asking identical questions about daydreaming of fame show no significant increase across the decades in the proportion of young people who say they do such daydreaming.

The surveys show that as age increases, there is a corresponding decline in daydreaming about fame and expectations of becoming famous. In some instances, this decline may be explained—at least in part—by history. For example, the extraordinary sequence of events that convulsed Germany in the dozen years from the rise to the fall of Adolf Hitler may well have discouraged Germans of all ages from any hope of becoming famous. Similarly, in China, Mao Tse-tung's cultural revolution may have done much the same. But the most likely reason why people's dreams of fame diminish as they grow older is that as the years available for becoming famous go by, reality sets in. One woman put it this way: "In my early twenties I knew I would be famous as a country western singer. When, at thirty-five, it was clear that I would not be famous as a singer—or in any other way—I found it very difficult to deal with but finally gave up hoping."

Education

They surveys show that even among Americans with less than a high school education, fully 45 percent dream of becoming famous, and fully 20 percent believe that they will get their fifteen minutes of fame. Yet the surveys document the association of education and visions of fame. They report that as education increases, so does dreaming about fame and expecting to achieve it. More education, usually coupled with more financial and social resources, encourages one to speculate about becoming famous. College graduates who make such speculations exceed, by about 20 percent, those with less than high school completion who do so. This was true in Germany and Beijing as well as in the United States.

Fame will always have to compete with other dreams more important to lower-income families. Asked in an interview whether he had any recollection of early interest in fame, a midlife male reported,

> That wasn't the driving force in my socialization. The driving force in my socialization is to get an education in order to get out of the coal patch town that I grew up in. And that's what my brothers learned as well. And the idea was not to become famous but, rather, to latch onto some enterprise that would guarantee that you would never have to be a coal miner.
>
> This is a way of thinking that would be so antithetical to the way in which my parents ever thought about the world. The way they thought about it is basically that the world comes to you in a kind of preformed packaged way, and your job is basically to find the best niche you can find for yourself that will make sure that you'll be able to provide for yourself and your family. So you don't think about inventing . . . all you think about doing is getting the credentials that will allow you to occupy such a niche. That's what you're thinking about.

Another interviewee, asked whether there was family conversation about being famous, said,

> Oh, God, no. I mean my father and mother were—they just had one year of college. Oh, God, no. They never, ever thought of that. It was too far beyond their reach. I mean, they'd just say, "I hope you become happy professionally, you want to be professor, you want to be a doctor, you want to be a lawyer." I almost became a lawyer because my uncle was a lawyer in a small town in New Jersey where I grew up. That was the hope. That you would be a professional, and you'd have a nice life, period. That's it. That's the end of the rainbow. The notion of being famous was never entertained at the dinner table. Because they started out so low, you know.

Summary

- Our beliefs and attitudes about fame and the fame motive range from passionate desire by a few, to indifference on the part of a vast majority, to aversion on the part of some.
- As we grow up in the subcultures of the United States and, later in life, assume adult social roles, we acquire different views about fame and the fame motive, especially about whether the fame motive can be openly expressed.
- Dreams and expectations about being famous exist in all parts of the population. They are greatest for younger, well-educated men and least for older, less-educated women. The differences are statistically significant but small.

4 ☆ A Tangled Web of Motives

The Familiar Trio: Fame, Money, and Power

Just as we have more than one goal in life, we have multiple motives, whose relationships with one another can vary from harmonious to conflicting and can often change with the passing of time. The fame motive is embedded in this complex mixture. We may want to be famous but rarely want it so intensely that other goals are excluded. An executive at IBM says he is very ambitious to make money, but in competitive ocean sailing—the Bermuda Gold Cup race—he is after fame.

In my study of the desire for fame, I found that the motives most likely to be coupled with it are those for money and power. As one interviewee said, "Sure. Fame. Add money and power . . . It's all one word." In this, he oversimplified, not distinguishing between fame as a means to an end and fame as an end in itself.

When fame is the ultimate goal and when money or power is employed to achieve it, the fame motive occurs in its primary form: power can lead to fame, and money can lead to fame. Should either such effort prove unsuccessful, a dedicated fame seeker will abandon it and try something else—as will be discussed in chapter 6.

Certain interviewees comments—"Of course, want to be famous so can have power" and "Of course, get famous to make money"—describe the opposite relationship, with power or money being the goal, while fame is seen as the way to achieve it. Fame can lead to power, and fame can lead to money. When fame is to be merely a stepping-stone to other goals, the

fame motive assumes its secondary form, in which it is not desired for itself and probably not caused by deprivation in early life. In this form, the
fame motive can emerge rapidly and develop at any point in a lifespan and
can disappear as quickly when its usefulness is over. Seeking fame can be
situational—done to meet a short-term goal, such as making enough
money to pay for a child's college education, and then abandoned.

Fame can also come unintended—perhaps not even wanted, but endured while it lasts—and with it may come money or power. In the film
Hero, actor Dustin Hoffman, playing the lead character, flees the site of his
heroic actions after an airplane crash, before fame, to which he is averse,
can fall on him. Later, he trades his potential fame for money by allowing
another to take credit for his heroics in exchange for financing his son's education.

That we often think of fame and money together is completely understandable. Examples of the connection are all around us. Endorsements by
Michael Jordan and Tiger Woods bring them millions of dollars. A hundred
lectures in a year do the same for Colin Powell. Hillary Clinton sold her
memoirs for eight million dollars. Ronald Reagan's generated three to five
million; those of Eisenhower and Lyndon Johnson, one million apiece.
Nixon received a million dollars for four TV interviews and a couple of
books on policy. (Ironically, in this era of big money, the champion of them
all died more than a century ago: Ulysses S. Grant's memoirs brought in
more than two million dollars, when the dollar was worth more than thirty
times what it is today.)

Sammy Glick, the antihero of Budd Schulberg's novel *What Makes
Sammy Run,* schemes to get his name in gossip columns, steals the ideas of
others and puts his name on them, and plots continuously to become famous. But his real goal—what truly makes him run—is money.[1] This is a
classic example in American literature of pursuing fame to achieve wealth.
In an interview, a school-age girl talked about "having her name up in
lights."

> There's something about it that's, like, larger than life, you know. Like
> this will be more than the standard American dream. This will mean
> that you're doing the most with your life. And not only will hundreds
> of people know your name, hundreds and thousands of people know
> who you are, and know that you're beautiful and spectacular and pop-
> ular, but you'll also have lots of money and fast cars and be able to go
> on vacation, and it doesn't really look like work. Because that's what it's

all about. You have millions and millions of dollars to do, like, really fun stuff. And basically play all day and get invited to parties.

It's also clear that fame can bring power. Especially in our era of mass media, people pay attention to what famous people say and do; even their most inane acts and comments are widely reported and often taken seriously. P. David Marshall, in his important study of celebrity and power, describes how fame in show business brings influence.[2] A woman being interviewed described the consequences of an article that made her famous.

> *Did it matter to you, in any way, that you as a person were being recognized? I understand that it would be very gratifying to feel that the work you did made a difference in people's lives. But would it have mattered if you had published it anonymously?*

> Oh, yes, I think so, because there were a lot of things that flowed from that. Just being invited to be one of the founders of the National Organization of Women was a direct consequence of that article and the fact that it hit many of the women who, like Friedan herself, were the prime movers who were calling for that first meeting in Washington, at the *Washington Post* headquarters. Yes, there were consequences that flowed from the public acknowledgment of the importance of that essay.

> *It made you famous, and so you have these consequences, but I think it didn't matter to you as a person that you'd become so well known except that it gave you more influence.*

> Yes, I could do more. It was opening doors to active political roles that I didn't expect. I was more concerned with influencing people's minds and their values, individuals out there in the larger society, and I hadn't expected and was in a sense surprised at the way in which that eventually opened the door to being asked to be on President Carter's commission on International Women's Year.

In another interview, a man described his role in creating the Internet.

> *Was there a turning point in your career when you realized that you were no longer famous?*

> Oh, yes.

And how did you feel about that?

Well, the loss of power was disconcerting. I could no longer make a statement and have an influence on what was going on. I had to prove myself again, and I couldn't catch up with what I was doing.

Are you less well known now than you used to be?

Yes, but it's coming back. It went like this, and all of a sudden the Internet exploded, and I went off to do other things simultaneously, so relative well-knownness went way down. But now it's starting to come back because I'm able to get involved again.

The power is coming back?

Well, at this point, it's just recognition. Not much power yet. I haven't established credibility.

Do you like that because it's a means to get power?

Right. Let's use the word *influence* instead of *power.*

Power has been alleged to be the ultimate aphrodisiac, but fame may be even greater. Fame, as we know, opens the door to rewards other than money and power: sex, for instance. Compared to other possible rewards, however, sex may be barely in the running. A national opinion poll conducted in 2000 asked respondents, "If you were famous, how would you be likely to use your fame?" Of the five choices given, one led the rest by a large margin. "To help others who are less fortunate than you are" was selected as "very likely" by 84 percent. (See "Preferred Uses of Fame.")

Individuals whose fame has been dedicated to attracting support for good works have become internationally known, even revered. Examples include Mother Teresa for her efforts among India's poor, Jane Goodall for her work with chimpanzees in Africa, and the Dalai Lama for his tours to promote world peace. When the fame motive assumes this secondary form, as a means to an end more highly prized, it may unexpectedly produce rewards of such value that it grows in importance and overwhelms or displaces the original goal, to become the goal itself. In the Victorian age, John Stuart Mill described this transformation.

> The strongest natural attraction, both of power and of fame, is the immense aid they give to the attainment of our other wishes; and it is the strong association thus generated between them and all our objects of

desire, which gives to the direct desire of them the intensity it often assumes so as in some characters to surpass in strength all other desires. In these cases the means have become a part of the end, and a more important part of it than any of the things which they are means to. What was once desired as an instrument for the attainment of happiness, has come to be desired for its own sake. In being desired for its own sake it is, however, desired as part of happiness. The person is made, or thinks he would be made, happy by its mere possession; and is made unhappy by failure to obtain it.[3]

Three Personality Characteristics Similar to the Fame Motive

Scholarly studies of human personality have isolated a wide variety of motives, needs, traits, and so on for analysis and explanation, but never the fame motive. The standard explanation for this is that the motive has been examined already as an individual's "need for achievement"—defined as "a wish to accomplish something difficult or to engage in competition against standards of excellence" and the like—about which much has been written.[4] In itself, however to "achieve" is a *general* desire, and it is *that* desire, its origins and hallmarks, which has been studied so extensively, rather than the goals to be achieved, which vary with individuals and might be anything from money or power to recognition by one's peers or even fame. The fame motive can also be confused with certain other characteristics that often coexist with it in a single personality. Three examples of this worth examining are individuality, narcissism, and the need for affiliation.

Individuality

Many well-known personality theorists (e.g., Abraham Maslow, Carl Jung, Karen Horney, Erich Fromm) write about "individuation and self-actualization" and the "inherent positive tendency for self-realization." In my view, these theories all point to the existence of a human characteristic that appears again and again in many ways and places. There seems to be no agreed-on name for it, and for the want of a better term, I'll simply call it the desire for individuality—with individuality defined as "the sum of the characteristics or qualities that set one person or thing apart from others" or "individual character . . . the condition of existing as an individual; separate existence."[5] This desire for individuality has two components: uniqueness and presence, which I think of as "I am me" and "I am here."

Although these components can be satisfied without the achievement of fame—through positive responses from the relatively small circle of an individual's family, friends, coworkers, community, and so on—they provide illuminating background for understanding the fame motive.

To start with uniqueness, here is an insight from C. R. Snyder and his colleagues, who have studied "uniqueness seeking."

> People have a need to be distinctive and special. Interpersonal difference, or uniqueness, contributes to self-identity, attracts attention, and enhances self-esteem and social status. On the other hand, people also have a need for similarity. Interpersonal similarity begets affiliation, belief-validation, emotional security, empathy, helping, liking, and social influence . . . Accordingly, people find a compromised position of intermediate levels of self-distinctiveness more satisfying than either extreme similarity or extreme dissimilarity relative to other persons.[6]

Everyone needs a sense of "I am me" and "the only one like me." In television commercials, the Equitable Life Insurance Company used to declare, "There is nobody else like you." Each of us is unique in some respect, but in truth, how unique are we? We share some characteristics with all humans and some with others in our culture, while some are ours alone. It's easy to overestimate the uniqueness of our personal attitudes and beliefs and values. We think that ours are idiosyncratic to ourselves, but we are often reminded that they're not.

In Sweden during World War II, babies and young children were moved from the cities to foster homes in the country to protect them from danger. Among them were many pairs of identical twins. Some years later, a search of government archives revealed that about 150 pairs never were told that they had an identical twin. To many, it was a major shock to their sense of their uniqueness to learn that there was another human exactly like themselves—like a sort of parallel universe where "another you" exists. Most sets of twins were intensely curious to meet each other and find out what that brother or sister had become, both no doubt searching or at least hoping for differences that would make themselves unique.[7]

The expression of one's uniqueness can take many forms and need not be validated or even recognized by others. For example, one may "seek uniqueness in our private and socially acceptable ways, such as acquiring rare and inconspicuous possessions." A strong motive for uniqueness has been found to correlate closely with a "desire for scarce products . . . [and] customized products"—that is, conspicuous consumption.[8]

While a unique achievement is usually the reason one becomes famous, this doesn't mean that people who are trying to be unique are also trying to become famous. They may have no interest in public recognition of their uniqueness and even try to avoid it. They can believe they are unique without outside confirmation. They consider themselves unique, in an inner life of thought, without outside confirmation. The fame motive is not there.

Now consider presence. As American GIs of World War II will remember, the phrase "Kilroy was here" was inscribed in tens of thousands of places around the world—on posters and village walls, in barracks and latrines—seemingly everywhere. There was no Kilroy, of course. The phrase simply stated, "I was here," whether the soldier who had passed that way added his name or not.

In the Tyne Cot cemetery near Ypres, Belgium, there are 11,908 graves, of which 70 percent are those of unidentified soldiers from World War I. On the walls are the names of 34,927 soldiers reported missing with no known graves. In an adjoining memorial area, propped up against a wall, is a sheet of paper, backed by wood and protected by plastic. Its message reads,

Lance Corporal Henry John Martin
Royal West Kent Regiment
Born Islington 14th October 1880

I was mobilised from the reserve in August 1914 and fought at St Ghislain, Mons, retreated down to the Marne, raced towards the sea via the Aisne and survived Neuve Chapelle despite being almost surrounded.

With *C* Company I helped to take Hill 60 on 17th April 1915, fought through 2nd Ypres and was wounded at High Wood, Somme on 22nd July 1916. I spent 14 months convalescing in Blighty only to return to Passchendaele and be blown to pieces at Poel Capelle on 27th November 1917.

I have no known grave, only my name on this panel and a plaque dedicated to me at St Georges Memorial Church, Ieper.

I did my best

Please remember me

The modest tone of this message finds an echo—coupled with good humor—in the Kilroy inscriptions.

Something quite different is conveyed in the explosion of graffiti in many cities and countries during recent decades. While some of it is creative and carefully executed—we speak of "graffiti artists"—most graffiti range from tasteless to menacing, not excluding outright vandalism. As with Kilroy, the spray-painting defacer of public buildings is asserting, "I was here. I'm putting my mark on the world." Chapter 6 describes how graffiti are seen as is a way to attain the fame. Fundamental to all of these examples is the natural urge to transcend and somehow overcome a condition where we are doomed to die and be forgotten and lost forever.

Narcissism

As noted earlier, references to fame or the fame motive are not to be found in standard texts on either personality or psychology in general. In psychiatry, however, there is more to consider. The American Psychiatric Association's *Diagnostic and Statistical Manual of Mental Disorders (DSM-IV)*[9] includes twelve pages of lists of various mental disorders. Among these are eleven "personality disorders":

paranoid	narcissistic	anti-social
schizoid	avoidant	borderline
schizotypal	dependent	histrionic
personality disorder	(not otherwise specified)	obsessive-compulsive

The descriptions of each of these include from six to ten characteristics of a person afflicted with the disorder. I found no references to the fame motive in any of them. In some, a single characteristic may refer to behavior that suggests the presence of the fame motive in the person being studied, but it will always be combined with a number of other characteristics that together define the disorder in question and therefore can't be considered proof of a desire for fame. All we can say is that the fame motive may well be a component of many different "personality types"—aggressive, shy, retiring, impulsive, controlled, and so on—without being of "Look at me!" intensity.

The narcissistic personality invites more attention. The self-loving youth Narcissus is commonly cited these days as an example of self-importance, a personality characteristic variously described in such comments as "Possessing a great need to be admired" and "Notable are the individual's exhibitionism and desire to gain attention and admiration from others" and "Despite the insouciant air of indifference and imperturbability, the individual is often quite preoccupied with how well he or she is regarded." Other descriptions are less sympathetic, even hostile. Havelock Ellis, in introducing the term *narcissism* in 1898, called it an "extortion in self-admiration." Descriptions of narcissism reviewed by Theodore Millon include "self-assured, arrogant, impressive in bearing, disdainful, and displaying airs of dignity and superiority," and having an admirable self-image, "e.g., confidently exhibits self, acting in a self-assured manner and displaying achievements; has a sense of high self worth, despite being seen by others as egotistic, inconsiderate, and arrogant."[10]

The *Narcissism Personality Inventory,* perhaps the best-regarded measure of narcissism in subclinical populations, identifies seven different narcissistic motives: authority, exhibitionism, superiority, entitlement, exploitativeness, self-sufficiency, and vanity. There is no mention of a fame motive.[11] As to the origin of narcissism, there are varied and contradictory speculations, some of them psychoanalytic. Freud has suggested that in the course of development, the child comes to avoid the mother as a primary love object and substitutes the self instead. Millon has a social-learning explanation: "The foundation of the disorder is best traced to excessive and unconditional parental valuation; this results in an unjustified sense of self-worth." Millon also writes that there has been minimal research concerning either specific criteria for narcissistic personality disorder or whether they cohere into a meaningful pattern: "The decision to introduce the narcissistic disorder into *DSM-III* [the earlier publication of the American Psychiatric Association, where the disorder was first included] was not received in an entirely favorable manner." Other scholars, George Valliant among them, have raised additional questions: "Developing and refining criteria that could be identified and reliably evaluated remain troublesome aspects of this disorder."[12]

As these opinions demonstrate, there is plenty of disagreement about both the cause and the exact nature of narcissism. My own conclusion is that among those exhibiting narcissistic behavior, there will be some who, through their constant need for unusual attention, can be identified as fame-motivated. In reverse, many fame seekers, most obviously those in the performing arts, are clearly narcissistic. The motive and the personality disorder may exist in the same person, but narcissism and the fame motive are not the same.

Need for Affiliation

The need for affiliation has been defined as a recurrent preference in thought and behavior for "establishing, maintaining, or restoring a positive . . . relationship with another person or persons." Those who score high on measurements of this need say that they "learn social relationships more quickly, or are more sensitive to faces than to other objects, engage in more dialogue with others, make more telephone calls, write more letters, pay more visits to friends, join more social clubs," and so on. In one study, students equipped with electronic pagers were beeped randomly throughout the day for a week. Those high in the need for affiliation were found to be talking with or writing a letter to someone more often than were low scorers: "They were significantly less often found to be alone."[13]

The need for affiliation resembles the fame motive in that it, too, can be aroused when one is deprived of acceptance and approval. This has been demonstrated by a number of experiments involving threats of rejection by peers (e.g., by reminding college students that they've been left out of being pledged to a fraternity). In measuring individual differences among respondents, investigators have found that those who score high in their need for affiliation are almost always among the least popular. Late-maturing boys, anxious about their masculinity, also score high. Common to all, however, is the fear of rejection.

Scholars studying the need for affiliation have not yet connected it to the desire for fame. Both motives, in my view, have such similar origins— fear of rejection (need for affiliation) and experience of rejection (fame)— that they must spring from a common root. If we were to investigate, I believe that many who score high on the affiliation motive would express a desire to become famous.

Summary

- In the primary form of the fame motive, fame is the only goal.
- In the secondary form, the achievement of fame is only a means to some other goal, such as money or power.
- Among the many motives, desires, and wishes that have been ascribed to human beings over the centuries, a small number can be confused with the fame motive: examples are individuality, narcissism, and the need for affiliation. Although they may coexist in personality with the fame motive, all three of these characteristics have different purposes and objectives.

Part Two ☆ **Choices, Challenges, Changes**

Introduction: Changes during the Life Course

The fame that a person dreams about and may attain will differ in whether name or face or voice (or two or all three of these) is famous. It will differ in the action that brings fame. It will differ in whether it is unintended or intended. It will differ in the size of the audience among whom people are famous, in how soon they are famous, and in how long it lasts. These are types of fame, according to where one falls along these dimensions and how they intersect and combine. A person might be famous in a small audience but have fame that occurred early in life and lasts a lifetime. For another, fame may be worldwide but come late and rapidly disappear.

I assume that a person seeking fame wants to have name, face, and voice recognition, to be world-famous at an early age, and to have it last forever. Yet for those who long for fame, only a few will be successful. Many more people who want to be famous will fail. To put some numbers on that assertion, let's play a game. In the United States, there are approximately three thousand Halls of Fame, from Cooperstown to the sidewalks of Hollywood Boulevard. Assuming that there are only fifty honorees per hall and that a third of them are deceased produces a total of one hundred thousand living men and women who are more or less famous. Adding one hundred thousand names from *Who's Who in the World* and other directories of the eminent doubles the total to two hundred thousand. Earlier in this book, I estimated the incidence of the fame motive in the U.S. adult population at about 2 percent, or four million individuals. If four million people have an inner drive to become famous and if only two hundred thousand have achieved fame—a large number of whom would have done so unintentionally, without the fame motive in their makeup—it is clear that well under 5 percent of fame-motivated individuals have much chance of having even a shred of their dreams come true.

Now that the game, with all its loose assumptions, is over, I will add a personal opinion: 5 percent is a wildly generous estimate. I would put their chances below 1 percent. My view is shared by Samuel Johnson, writing in 1751 about fame and obscurity: "How little vacancy is left in the world for any new object of attention; to how small extent the brightest blaze of merit can be spread amidst the mists of business and folly; and how soon it is clouded by the intervention of other novelties."[1] One can speculate that the chances of becoming famous may be no worse than the chances of becoming rich or a best-selling novelist, but people who fail at those endeavors can give them up and try something else.

Imagine that a person looks ahead and envisions the tens of thousands of life events to be confronted from childhood to death. There will be biological events that, among others, encompass developmental changes in body size and bone structure, in the endocrine system, in the brain and central nervous system, in susceptibility to various diseases and finally to organ failures. Add to these the customary events of family life, work, community, religion, friendship, introduction to sex, marriage, starting a family, becoming independent of parents, establishing a home, changing an occupation in midlife, taking on civic and social responsibilities, accepting retirement, caring for aging parents, dealing with the death of a spouse. There well may be negative events as well, including crimes against one's person, being cheated, being lied about, being derogated, physical fights, extramarital affairs, and divorce.

Unpredictable events in the physical world may also have to be endured, such as earthquake, injury from accident, the destruction of one's home by fire. There are internal or psychological events as well. These may include religious experience and conversion, such as being "born again"; the resolution to devote one's life to a cause greater than self; the decision to leave one's spouse; the pride and disappointment in recognizing that one has reached the apex of one's career; the confrontation with one's own mortality at midlife; fathers' acceptance that their sons may turn out to be stronger and more successful than themselves; mothers' acceptance that their daughters may be more competent and attractive than they are; and the regret that, on balance, one may have done more harm than good to others.[2]

As these events accompany or succeed one another in the course of a fame seeker's life, all but the already famous few will see the images of themselves as famous blur and fade. But these images will not die. Instead, they will be replaced by new images, as fame seekers try new ways to become famous or (more likely) lower their sights—from total recognition to perhaps just their names, from the desire for a grand audience to being known to a relative few. They may alter their inner timetables in the hope that fame will come later in life, or they may lower their aspirations from lasting fame to just a few days or even hours. They may struggle to give up the goal of becoming famous, but I doubt that, deep down, they ever really do.

The following chapters describe changes in the expression of the fame motive through life, with the final chapter devoted to what happens when one faces the final reality: that one is as famous as one will ever be. As the reader must already be aware, it is my view that although the realities of life over time may cause a person seeking fame to give up or greatly modify the image of fame originally pursued, the motive itself will remain. This would seem to conflict with one of the basic principles in psychology: that a given behavior eventually disappears—"extinguishes"—if it is not followed by a reward. But that's not to say that if a motive is not rewarded, then the motive extinguishes. Behavior enlisted to reach a goal may change in response to failure, while the desire for the goal may continue as before.

This leads directly to one of the fundamental and complicated issues in all of psychology: to what degree can personality change? In an earlier book, *Ambition,* I wrote,[3]

Each age and place has its own theories of human nature in the form of myth, legend, and religious belief. Such theories deal with the goodness or evil of humankind, with what is inherited and what is learned, and with whether humans are dominant over, subjected to, or simply part of nature. The possibilities of human metamorphosis are present in the classic tales in Western civilization in our popular literature, ranging from the great myths and legends of the past to their counterparts in television, film, magazines, newspapers, and fiction and nonfiction of the present time. Our treasured stories about metamorphosis in children—*Alice in Wonderland, Pinocchio, Snow White, Peter Pan*—are especially poignant because they engage children's fascination with transformation of self. A representative group of well-known tales might begin with the pre-Egyptian legends of Osiris, continue through Ovid's *Metamorphoses* and the story of Paul's conversion to Christianity on the road to Damascus.

Students of human behavior have argued for a century that it's difficult to change our personalities, which are lastingly affected by our experience of early childhood. Each discipline has its own reason for insisting that childhood is critical. Psychologists argue that it's difficult to rid ourselves of behavior learned in our early years, because it became part of us before we were old enough to understand how and why we learned it. Psychiatrists and psychoanalysts believe that we never resolve intense childhood conflicts but only find new ways to deal with them—essentially, by developing new defenses and evasions. Sociologists have told us that the ways we classify and label our children—dumb, smart, ugly, beautiful—produce self-images in them that may last through life. Pediatricians and other physicians believe that because nutrition affects physical growth, poor nutrition in childhood may permanently affect how well the brain works in adult life.

Other scholars of human development—I am one of them—have advanced the idea that it's possible for fundamental inner change to occur. We have questioned the traditional idea that the experiences of childhood outlive their contemporaneous effects, to shape and constrain the characteristics of adolescence and adulthood. In this new view of development, although our early years are influential, we have a capacity for change throughout life; just as there are important physical changes from birth to death, many individuals have an accompanying capacity for inner change, so that the consequences of the events of early childhood are continually transformed by later experiences, making the course of human development more open and less foreordained than many have believed.

The proper question about lifespan development is not whether people change or do not change; everyone changes, but some more than others and in different ways. The right question is, what are the conditions that cause some of us to change in certain ways while others stay the same? This is not to deny the importance of antecedent childhood experiences but, rather, to say that new experiences in midlife are added, are mixed into the stream, and create new trajectories of development.

The principal studies of change have centered on personality traits and changes in behavior. A truly vast amount of research exists on how traits persist over time, with concentration on what are termed the "Big Five," most commonly referred to these days as extroversion, agreeableness, conscientiousness, neuroticism, and openness to experience.[4] Many studies have demonstrated the considerable stability and continuity of these traits in individuals over substantial periods of time. Their capacity to endure supports the theory that they're genetically based.

Many studies of efforts to change behavior also exist—as many as a thousand on attempted weight control, for instance. It is a popular belief not only that humans can change but also that we can change ourselves. The unending stream of self-help books, self-help advice in magazines and newspapers, and self-help advertisements on television and radio all stand as proof that many millions of Americans are trying to change themselves day by day, trying to be different, trying to be something more than they are now. Martin Seligman reviews this work, which includes attempts to revitalize your marriage, reshape your body, resolve your sexual hang-ups, give up smoking, and more.[5] The continuing abundance and persistence of these appeals show how difficult it is for people to make these changes. Even when they resort to therapy, which has proved effective in addressing such problems, it's questionable whether one's personality or merely one's behavior is changed. Psychotherapy can address depression and single symptoms, such as anxiety, with highly positive results, but personality structure may not be basically altered.

Important as these areas of research undoubtedly are, they have not yet addressed what, in my view, are the most important elements of personality: namely, our beliefs about what is good and what is true and our beliefs about ourselves, our motives, and our goals. Research on major changes in motives over several decades of a lifetime—and particularly on the related internal processes that bring them about—is almost impossible to find. Psychologist Heinz Heckhausen asked some years ago whether anybody has studied what happens to goals that people claim to have pursued five or ten years previously. My own view is that one will withdraw energy and interest and attention from a goal-seeking effort if it becomes harder and harder to make progress or overcome setbacks, with lower self-esteem as a consequence, and will begin to shift direction toward a seemingly more reachable goal of acceptable value, with higher self-esteem as a by-product. To resolve the inevitable discrepancies between aspiration and achievement, many readjustments may be necessary; goals may need to be shifted or redefined downward. Occasionally, an entire area of activity may be abandoned for one that appears more promising.

We are in strange territory here. The path of life is full of twists and turns; what happens to people's deep-seated motives through these vicissitudes—how they wax, wane, mutate, or simply fade away—is unknown to science. Perhaps they can be changed, suppressed, repressed, sublimated, transformed, even eliminated. We have yet to find out. The research, once it occurs—and it will—should illuminate numerous questions of widespread interest and importance. Does the desire for money increase or decrease over the life span, and under what circumstances does it do so? Does the power motive ever disappear? Is the motive for altruism formed in childhood or only when the individual is mature enough to be aware of social conditions and the need for good works? Am I right in believing that the fame motive can never be satisfied?

In earlier writings, I have set forth my belief in the possibility of personality change with reference to a range of desires and motives. The motive for fame, in my view, is different. How it is expressed may change—perhaps often—during an individual's lifetime, but for the millions of people with the fame motive in their makeup, it will never be fully satisfied. It's also clear that the strength of the fame motive varies greatly from person to person. This leads to different intensity levels of behavior, with stronger motives generating the stronger actions of the kind I describe in subsequent chapters. This doesn't mean that a weaker desire for fame is more easily satisfied. At whatever level of strength fame may be achieved, it is never enough to satisfy the fame seeker, much less cause the fame motive to disappear.

5 ☆ The Source of Fame

Fame exists because, as humans, we pay attention to differences. Research in psychology on "variability discrimination" shows that we are intrigued by the unusual. Fame will be given to the exceptional person but not to the ordinary.

A friend observed that as soon as you pay attention to any characteristic, such as size, you note the people at the extremes of the distribution (i.e., some people are small, while others are big). It's those people whom you talk about. Someone is famous, then, because he's the tallest man on record or the shortest. No other distinguishing mark is needed to bring fame. In fact, almost any marked departure from the norm in any walk of life will do, at least briefly.

Consider for a moment what society would be like if fame did not exist. This kind of speculation goes by the impressive name of *counterfactual thought experiments*. Examples might include "Had Pontius Pilate pardoned Jesus, what would have happened?" or "What might the incredible Chinese navy have accomplished in the Atlantic and the New World had the Ming emperors not turned inwards and ordered the destruction of China's fleets of sailing ships?"

As an analogy for fame, let's choose alcohol. Suppose there were a society where there is no alcohol, where it never existed. Clearly, alcoholism would never surface. Similarly, in a society where fame is unknown, the unfilled need that some people have for acceptance and approval could not be expressed through the search for fame, and another solution would have to be sought.

Ironically, in the modern world, fame has become so transitory that, in some ways, it hardly exists. Of the billions of human beings alive today, most were born since 1920, and very few of them remember famous persons from earlier than 1910. By the end of the twenty-first century, few will remember celebrities of the 1980s or '90s. In today's information explosion, many forms of communication in many languages have become commonplace around the globe. This tremendous apparatus's appetite for names and news to pass on is seemingly infinite.

Hence, almost anything can be famous. A tree can be famous for its height, a river for its flooding, a painting for being stolen, a dog for inheriting a fortune. An Internet search for "famous Chinese" listed famous quotations, famous garden landscapes, famous traditional Chinese medicine cures, famous tours of China, famous Chinese paintings. When it came to people, the one and only entry was "Chinese beauties and pop stars."

A person can be famous for a single act (Nathan Hale), for being rich (King Croesus), or even for a body part (Achilles' heel, Jimmy Durante's nose). Helen Keller is renowned for overcoming deafness and blindness, Henry VIII for practicing serial monogamy, Dr. Jack Kevorkian for advocating assisted suicide. As dramatic as a rise to fame can be, there is equal fascination when the mighty fall, as in the cases of Julius Caesar, Napoleon, and Hitler.

The allocation of fame is a complex social process. Unlike wealth and power, which can be acquired through one's own efforts, fame is an attribute bestowed by others; without the approval—or at least the awareness—of a relevant audience, it won't exist. Not only is fame elusive, there is also no straight path to it. On any path to fame, one will encounter plenty of obstacles, wrong turns, and dead ends, some of which are worth examining:

1. Fame is not fair.

2. One can be fated to be in the wrong time and/or place.

3. Infamy exists—society notes evil acts as well as the benign.

4. Much fame was never sought or intended.

Fame Is Not Fair

Fama is a goddess in Greek and Roman mythology who personified fame. It's surprising to learn that the Greeks regarded her as an evildoer. To quote

Braudy, "the historical evidence demonstrates quite clearly that fame has, to some extent, always been regarded as essentially amoral and frequently undeserved."[1] In *The House of Fame,* written in the fourteenth century, Chaucer presents Fame as arbitrary, irrational, and fickle. He gives her the alternative name of Rumour and, toward the end of the poem, associates her with the bearers of false tidings: sailors, pilgrims, pardoners, and messengers, the riffraff of Chaucer's day.

As we know, not all achievements of merit are recognized by fame. Even after making contributions of great value to society, many people die obscure. The editors of a collection of obituaries prepared for the *New York Times* report that many of those receiving lengthy write-ups are "folks whose names we wouldn't recognize but whose accomplishments we do." They explain further, "Thus among the doctors we included the physician who pioneered the mammogram as a tool against breast cancer. Few know his name, but all over America women now get mammograms."[2]

Some people are famous for happenings never intended to bring fame. Since food and clothing are universal necessities, a sure mark of fame is to have one's name on an article of apparel or choice bit of cuisine. For reasons unknown, opera stars and English generals of the nineteenth century have been especially favored. Among the many examples are the following:

- Chicken or turkey Tetrazzini (with pasta, mushrooms, almonds, and Parmesan cheese)—named for Italian-born Luisa Tetrazzini (1874–1940), a world-class coloratura of the early twentieth century, often cast opposite Caruso in *Rigoletto, La Traviata,* and other operas.
- Peach Melba—named for Australian-born Nellie Melba (1861–1931), the most famous diva of her day. Created in her honor by Auguste Escoffier, chef of the Ritz Hotel in London, it consists of half a ripe peach (Melba was partial to peaches) on a bed of vanilla ice cream, topped with the juice of fresh raspberries and, for the self-indulgent, whipped cream.
- Cardigan sweater (knitted of wool and buttoning up the front)—supposedly invented by James Thomas Brudenell, 7th Earl of Cardigan, the reckless soldier who led the Charge of the Light Brigade in the Crimean War.
- Raglan sleeve—named for Fitzroy James Henry Somerset, 1st Baron Raglan (1788–1855). A British commander in chief in Crimea, he had lost an arm at Waterloo, and the loose-fitting shoulder construction

worked up by his tailor made it easier for the stump to fit in and out of an overcoat.

The *Book of Lists* presents some "little-known inventors of common things": "Margaret Knight—Flat-bottomed Paper Bag (1869); Joseph Glidden—Barbed Wire (1874); William Painter—Crown Bottle Cap (1892); Whitcomb L. Judson—Zipper (1893); Jacques Brandenberger—Cellophane (1908); Rose Cecil O'Neill—Kewpie Doll (1909); Georges Claude—Neon Sign (1910); Wallace Hume Carothers—Nylon (1934); Carlton Magee and Gerald Hale—Parking Meter (1935); Sylvan Goldman—Shopping Cart (1937); Chester Carlson—Xerographic Copier (1938); Robert Abplanalp—Aerosol Valve (1949)."[3]

In contrast, some people are famous for something they never did. A nine-year-old girl was credited by the children in her grade at school for saying something original that she actually had heard on television. The attention made her feel guilty, but she kept it to herself for more than a year before telling her mother. In a conversation I had with a scholar about his receiving one of the highest honors that his country can bestow on a scientist or artist, he said, "I am famous for something I don't deserve." Schopenhauer wrote,

> This is . . . what happens in the case of false, that is, unmerited, fame; . . . its recipient lives upon it without actually possessing the solid substratum of which fame is the outward and visible sign . . . [T]he time may come when . . . he will feel giddy on the heights which he was never meant to climb, or look upon himself as spurious coin; and in the anguish of threatened discovery and well-merited degradation, he will read the sentence of posterity on the foreheads of the wise—like a man who owes his property to a forged will.[4]

Some beneficiaries of undeserved fame may be less conscience-stricken. It is said that the explorer Richard E. Byrd deliberately falsified his diaries in claiming he had reached the North Pole; he had not.[5] As for the fame-seeking mountaineer Maurice Hertzog, the question has been raised whether he really did conquer the challenging summit of Mount Annapurna.[6]

Powerful social forces can arbitrarily bestow fame. One involves symbols. Selecting a famous person to symbolize a cause or an occupation or a category of achievement simplifies what otherwise might be complicated and makes it easier for us to take in. Clive James, in his book *Fame in the*

20th Century, says that we all need to know at least "one person who can comprehend what we can't" and that "it might as well be Einstein." He continues,

> We all need to know the name of at least one person who can sing the way we can't . . . It might as well be Pavarotti. We all need to know the name of at least one person who is good the way we aren't. It might as well be Mother Teresa . . . It does us no harm that Hitler is our ready symbol of a man more evil than we are, Lindbergh of a man more brave, the young Marlon Brando of a man more beautiful. It does us good.[7]

A second cause of the unfairness of fame are judges who select the famous. They serve as society's agents, telling the public who is noteworthy. A few can be identified: those who select the winners in organized contests, such as entry to Halls of Fame, Nobel Prizes, honorary degrees, and the annual awards of Oscars, Emmys, Tonys, and other show-business trophies. Also identifiable are the moguls of print and broadcast media and the journalists on their payrolls, who decide what is to be selected for reporting to the public. More limited spheres of fame control include book publishers, owners of art galleries, and disc jockeys, among others. In an amusing note on journalists as gatekeepers, Braudy writes: "Critical to the dissemination of such fame was therefore these new professionals on the American scene—the journalists almost immediately nominated themselves as intermediaries between their readers and those they wrote about, . . . like so many Dantes deciding who should be allocated to Hell, Purgatory, or Heaven."[8]

Where judges are involved, the complaint of the fame seeker that fame is not fair is often understandable. In a complex society, there will be plenty of disagreement about what is exceptional and worth publicity, and there will be many bad judgments, too. Sociologist William J. Goode, in a section of his book *The Celebration of Heroes* called "The Problem of the Judges," notes, "Where there are judges, both their competence and their character may be questioned," and "Doubtless, the problem of the judges has existed from the time the first contest prize was ever given, perhaps thousands of years ago." Goode goes on to describe how judges' feelings about what they like and don't like are quite variable and perhaps not even known to themselves.[9]

The current process of judging who are the winners among the thousands of prizes being awarded today is faulted by James F. English, who points out that extraordinary achievements often are overlooked or rated down. One can claim unfairness for this reason and also that the judges themselves, whether contest judges or media gatekeepers, can be corrupted. The fame seeker's adherents—whether few or many—can lobby secretly or publicly for their candidate and often succeed.[10]

In a unique instance of challenging the judges, Raymond Damadian protested the award of the Nobel Prize in Medicine for the year 2000, asserting that he should have been included. In two full-page advertisements in the *New York Times,* one headed "The Shameful Wrong That Must be Righted," he argued his own case for recognition. Much discussion followed, in newspapers and other media—was Damadian right or wrong to challenge the Nobel Committee?—accompanied by lists of extraordinary men and women who clearly deserved a Nobel Prize but did not receive it. The committee did not change its judgment.

A third cause of unfairness is that publicity intrudes. Persons seeking fame will promote public attention by their own efforts. As one might expect, there is no shortage of how-to and do-it-yourself books on how to start being famous in two weeks or less. Among the topics in such books are "How to Get There from Here," "Prepare Your Road Map to Fame," "Getting Your Act Together Before You Take It on the Road," "The Eight Gateways to Fame" (television, newspapers, radio, wire services, newsletters, the Internet, computer libraries, and databases), and "The Tools of the Trade and How to Use Them."[11] First, these books tell readers, you have to get attention through news, books, and story angles. Fame seekers may engage others to do this for them. According to the Bureau of Labor Statistics, there are more than 155,000 publicists in the United States.

The publicity may be untrue. For many years in the early nineteenth century, in the United States, P. T. Barnum produced and intensely promoted "The Greatest Show on Earth," a traveling production that continued for many years with immense success by presenting to the public a revolving collection of people—unique in their heights, weights, shapes, and deformities (e.g., bearded women and India-rubber men)—many of whom were fakes. In the late 1930s, at Phillips Academy in Andover, Massachusetts, a student managed to enter on the school records a fictitious classmate named A. Montague Fitzpatrick. When Fitzpatrick failed to show up for the classes he was scheduled to attend and other school appointments, the authorities became increasingly irritated by these repeated breaches of discipline and, in morning assembly, kept ordering the elusive student to report himself immediately. These demands from on high were greeted with rising levels of stifled laughter from students in the know, until, after a few days, the authorities caught on. Several years ago, at a reunion for students of the 1930s, returning Andover alumni were greeted with a sign that read, "Welcome to the A. Montague Fitzpatrick Alumni Center." A 2008 student wrote a paper about the prank, and so Fitzpatrick lives on.

Time and Place

Even in sports, where extraordinary achievement almost always leads to fame, significant national and cultural variations can exert themselves; one can be world-famous except in one's own country. When the runner Michael Johnson set a new four-hundred-meter world record, he was watched on television all over the world except in the United States, where his feat was preempted by a rerun of auto racing. Table tennis, an obscure sport in the United States, is a national passion in China.

Consider the case of Norman Borlaug, one of three American winners of the Nobel Peace Prize who were living in 1997.

> Though barely known in the country of his birth, elsewhere in the world Norman Borlaug is widely considered to be among the leading Americans of our age . . . He received the Nobel in 1970, primarily for his work in reversing the food shortages that haunted India and Pakistan in the 1960s . . . The form of agriculture that Borlaug preaches may have prevented a billion deaths.[12]

Our opinions about who and what are more or less deserving of fame not only differ by society but also change over time. What will people be famous for in 2050, in 2100? Lewis H. Lapham, the renowned editor of *Harper's Magazine*, explains that clergymen were esteemed in the 1700s, politicians in the 1800s, and scientists and novelists in the 1900s.[13] Richard M. Huber, a social analyst, wrote in his book *The American Idea of Success*, "It was the mass media, beginning in the 1920s with print going to radio, the movies, and phonograph records, later expanded by television, which created our Idols of Entertainment . . . In the 19th century fame was a reward for meeting certain basic needs of society—governing or protecting the nation. The dimension that has been added is fame by entertaining people."[14] In the late 1920s and early '30s, the people profiled in American magazines did indeed change from politicians, inventors, and entrepreneurs to entertainers. Tyler Cowen cites three polls on the changing nature of fame and reports a similar finding: that entertainers and sports figures have displaced politicians, military leaders, and preachers as the most famous individuals in the United States.[15]

Unquestionably chance—good or bad luck and being in the right place at the right time—plays an important part in the achievement of fame. A common contention in science is that no discovery is exclusive to an individual, that the growth of science is orderly and inexorable, so that if one scientist fails to make a needed discovery another will do so in ten or twenty years. Thus, the discoverer of a new scientific truth owes less to insight than to position in history.[16]

From Marco Polo through Columbus and Cortez to Amundsen, fame has been generous to explorers. A biography of Henry Morton Stanley ("Doctor Livingston, I presume") traces how his search for acceptance, fame, and admiration through extensive explorations in Africa stemmed from deep-seated feelings of inferiority and insecurity. Braudy notes, though, that as the world has become ever more charted and known, its few unexplored places are even more dangerous and expensive to penetrate, and exploration is no longer an easy path to fame.[17] As if that weren't enough, exploration has also been downgraded by historical revisionists, who disapprove of it as intrusive and destructive of indigenous cultures.

During the late 1880s, when packs of cigarettes contained colored cards of police captains, dancing girls, and baseball players, one brand included a series of fifty American editors. Today the editors have disappeared. The *Guinness Book of Records,* in a similar determination to stay contemporary, also has dropped categories that it viewed as obsolete. The man from India with the longest fingernails in the world is no longer considered famous. In short, no matter how hard one tries, success or failure in the quest for fame often depends on matters entirely beyond one's control. Fame is indeed unfair.

Infamy

Society awards fame to the extraordinary, not necessarily the worthy. Society, in fact, can be perversely intrigued by evildoers and almost any out-of-the-ordinary event that is considered—to borrow from a thesaurus—"terrible, dreadful, awful, horrible, atrocious, outrageous, villainous, nefarious, monstrous, scandalous, detestable, despicable, contemptible."[18] Milton writes,

> Fame, if not double fac'd, is double mouth'd,
> And with contrary blast proclaims most deeds;
> On both his wings, one black, the other white,
> Bears greatest names in his wild aery flight.[19]

William J. Goode writes, more prosaically,

> A distinction is both simple and operationally clear, however much they overlap concretely. People (or organizations) are more or less famous if they are known to many or few; they enjoy more or less esteem if people respect them more or less. Ordinary people can easily make this distinction between being well known and being well thought of, and often they do. They have, after all, heard of famous scoundrels.[20]

Most of the exceptional actions that bring fame are viewed by society as good or at least acceptable. Because infamous deeds are relatively rare, they not only have extra news value but shock value as well. Learning about them allows us to experience the thrill of contemplating evil from the comfortable perch of our own moral superiority. The delicious headiness of mixing good with evil was recognized by *Time* magazine when, in inviting people who had appeared on the magazine's cover to its seventy-fifth birthday party, it included the good and the bad, the famous and the infamous. Similarly, a book about the famous listed Whittaker Chambers and Lee Harvey Oswald along with Abraham Lincoln and Thurgood Marshall. *Fame at Last,* a collection of obituaries from the *New York Times,* listed reviews of the lives of college professors, financial executives, actors and actresses, inventors, and forty-one criminals. The editors classify the criminals by type of offense: spies and political crime, white-collar crime, organized crime, mafia, murderers, and "other crime."[21]

To be fascinated by evildoers is part of our culture: Cain, Delilah, and Herod in the Bible; Macbeth, Iago, and Richard III in Shakespeare; Benedict Arnold, John Wilkes Booth, and Osama bin Laden in American history. Braudy, writing about William Caulfield, the creator of *Black Guardiana; or, A Dictionary of Rogues* (1795), says, "Through his pages parade famous midwives and famous prostitutes, famous pickpockets and famous rag pickers."[22] More recently (1992), we have *The Oxford Book of Villains,* running to more than four hundred pages. In the new reality television, on Court TV, "a homeless man describes a rape, a male prostitute . . . his murder of a wheelchair bound client," while "another man admits killing a woman . . . and dismembering her."[23] Furthermore, trading cards of today depart sharply from those of the nineteenth century, cited earlier. Cards presenting famous murderers are among the best sellers.

As we see all the time, a single individual or action can be both famous and infamous, depending on the audience. In politics, polarizing personalities and events are so commonplace that no examples are needed, while political crimes are often the stuff of history. The judges who were honored for condemning King Charles I of England to be beheaded in 1649 had to flee for their lives when the monarchy was restored in 1660. Suicide bombers reviled by the Israelis are celebrated by their fellow Palestinians. The gender wars are recalled in an interview with a social scientist.

There must have been times when you had considerable public recognition of your role.

Yes, I think that, well, what were the instances of that? Um, I think of the response to my very first publication on sex equality. I was just amazed by the amount of feedback to that from people I didn't know at all who saw it as an intellectual counterpart to Friedan's book *The Feminine Mystique* and highly controversial. I mean reaction was completely polarized, either hating it or loving it.

My husband got consolation cards because he had such a ridiculous infamous wife, upstart, disturbing, ruffling the waters. After we made our debut as a feminist caucus about nine months later, I met in another context a graduate student from a midwest university whose professor came back from that meeting and was describing this ridiculous woman who was six-and-a-half feet tall, had green hair, and smoked cigars. That was me, supposedly. And she was shocked to find that I was five [feet] seven and brunette and I smoked cigarettes, not cigars.

Another interviewee said,

You can see the same person in some sections of society being famous and in other sections of society infamous. Recently, during this past year, I was reading biographies of some of the Rockefellers or the Fords, and you go back to the time when some parts of the press were nothing but praiseworthy, but there was another press dominated by progressive thoughts that saw these people as demons. They were exploiting workers. There were body-bag images in the cartoons and papers. Fame and infamy can be attached to the same individuals, depending on your underlying ideology.

Unintended Fame

Most persons who become famous weren't seeking fame but happened to capture attention for doing something else. To those with the fame motive, this kind of unintended consequence, if they happen to know about it, can be deeply frustrating. A friend who desperately wants fame commented to me, "I don't see why those who want it can't get it and those who don't care about it do get it—have it forced upon them, even. It doesn't seem fair." Jonathan Imber, a scholar of fame and recognition, says in a personal communication, "A figure such as Edward Bernays [widely recognized as the father of public relations] helped to change fundamentally the way in which judgment is accomplished, establishing as he did the idea of consciously helping to put something or someone before the public eye, indeed, creating that eye in some sense, too. It seems, too, in this way, that many instances of unintended fame are the result of this larger culture and technical process by which someone or something must be put out there each and every day (even hour) or there would be a lot of people with nothing to do, and fewer jobs in the media industry."

On September 11, 2001, United Airlines Flight 93 was hijacked by radical Islamists whose presumed plan was to divert it to Washington, D.C., and crash it into the White House or the Capitol. The passengers confronted the hijackers and forced the plane to crash into a field in Pennsylvania. All aboard lost their lives. Books have been written about this heroic event, several television shows have been produced, and a film has been made. The central figure in all of them is one Todd Beamer, who led the passenger revolt. Like most of us, he had no claim to fame until that day, when fame claimed him.

Not all unintended fame is glorious, of course. Jim Larson became famous because he lost his sister and his wife to murderers, seven years apart. The sister was stabbed to death by a serial killer in 1990, and his wife was abducted and her body found later in a shallow grave. As the common element in two extraordinary tragedies, Jim Larson became a celebrity.

The reaction of a person who becomes famous unintentionally can be indifference or aversion. James Bradley, in his book *Flags of Our Fathers* (later a film), tells of the celebrated flag raising on Iwo Jima late in World War II. The photograph of that event became famous around the world. One of the six men shown in it was the author's father, John Bradley. The son writes, "But that's all we knew. Our father himself never mentioned the photograph. He didn't encourage anyone else to mention it. No copies of it existed in the house . . . His Navy Cross he kept out of sight; none of us knew he had been awarded it until after he had died."[24]

The companion to unintended fame is unintended infamy, where an event you'd like to conceal attracts attention you'd hoped to avoid. This unwanted sequence had to be endured by Sidney Biddle Barrows, an entrepreneur of blue-blooded lineage who ran an upscale call-girl business that brought her to public attention as the "Mayflower Madam." Some lawbreakers like to mug for the news cameras. Not this woman of breeding. She never wanted to be famous.

As infamy can be unintended, it can also be undeserved. A case in point is that of Warren M. Anderson, a distinguished American business leader and CEO of Union Carbide, who was personally blamed for an industrial disaster suffered by his company on the other side of the world. A newspaper photograph of a large crowd of Indian marchers carrying a twenty-five-foot effigy of Warren Anderson is captioned, "Demonstrators March Effigy of Warren Anderson through Streets of Bhopal on Saturday." The text says: "Hundreds of women whose husbands died in the world's worst industrial accident burned straw-and-bamboo effigies Saturday of Warren Anderson. Children beat the burning figures with sticks as elders, many with tears in their eyes, shouted 'Death to Anderson'"[25] The cause of the disaster, which took many lives, were leaks from lethal gases and liquids stored in Union Carbide's chemical plant, one of the largest in the world—probably the result of anti-American sabotage. It cost the company billions of dollars.

Sports provide some lighter examples of infamy. In the 1929 Rose Bowl game, the University of California center, Roy Riegels, recovered a fumble and ran sixty-five yards in the wrong direction before a teammate managed to tackle him. As a consequence, Georgia Tech won the game by one point. Chuck Knoblaugh was a New York Yankee second baseman notorious for his wild throws to first base. Al Smith, a Chicago White Sox outfielder, "became the hapless subject in one of baseball's most famous photographs when a fan spilled a cup of beer on him."[26]

More recently, one Steve Bartman reached out from his grandstand seat to catch a foul ball that Moisés Alou, a Chicago Cubs outfielder, would certainly have caught. No out was scored, and from that point, things unraveled so completely for the Cubs that they lost the game—in which they had been leading—and ultimately the National League playoff. From an account by notable sportswriter Ira Berkow, "Bartman . . . was showered with abuse, with obscenities and beer, and was escorted by security out of Wrigley Field, his jacket covering his face as if he were on a perp walk."[27] Steve Bartman is not popular in Chicago. Cubs fans don't forget.

Summary

- Fame has its origin in the recognition of individual differences.
- In many instances, the awarding of fame is not fair.
- Fame depends on the time and place where the action occurs. There are many historical changes and cultural differences in what will receive fame.
- Recognition by society is not only for meritorious actions. Fame is bestowed for extraordinary actions, and these may be either good or evil.
- Most persons who become famous did not seek fame. For them, fame was an unintended consequence of a certain action, and the fame motive was not involved.

6 ☆ Finding a Path

We take many paths to achieve our goals. We may plan, scheme, contrive, devise, invent, even destroy. A person who wants to be wealthy plans how to make money. A person who wants power schemes how to get elected. Similarly, a person who wants to be famous will choose a path to fame. In this chapter, I describe four such paths:

1. a high level of honor where fame comes from achievements greatly valued by society;
2. fame by association with families and acquaintances;
3. acts made only to call attention to oneself, having no other purpose; and
4. strange and deviant acts that gain notice and usually result in infamy.

The actions we take during these quests, if we are fortunate, are those that on balance make us happy. They're also shaped by our intelligence, by the social rules we have learned or others enforce on us, by our beliefs about our capacities, by our experience of past events. We schedule and organize. We try to see beyond current problems and difficulties to where opportunity may lie. All this information and much more—changes inside and outside our immediate orbits, for example—we continually process and store and retrieve.

An informed source has a contradictory view: that most people are unsure of what they're doing and that many of us simply don't have long-term life goals but veer from one objective to another, adapting as we succeed or fail. We look for doors to open, slip through them, and in the next room look for another door. But which door should it be? Perhaps we should stay right here or even go back to the previous room, where we might have overlooked something. Some people prefer to avoid making choices, much less put together a plan. They drift into a course of action as it suggests itself in their lives. This is the opportunistic path to fame.

Actress Katherine Hepburn once remarked, "When I started out I didn't have any desire to be an actress or to learn how to act. I just wanted to be famous." A twenty-six-year-old reporter, one of the leaders of his generation, says that he "just wanted to be famous" before he was twenty-five—he didn't care what at. Novelist Salmon Rushdie said in an interview, "A graduating class of high school kids [in England] was asked what they wanted to be, and something like three-quarters of them answered that they wanted to be famous. I mean, as if that were a career. Famous for what didn't occur to them . . . anything would do. Performing a blow job on a president or murdering your wife. Albert Schweitzer or Monica Lewinsky, same thing. It is the curse of our time."[1]

Levels of Honor

The quest for fame can lead to actions from the trivial to the destructive: from obtrusive singing at parties, making drunken dinner speeches, or wearing odd-looking clothes in order to impress those we know, to deliberate murders of famous people in order to impress the world. Most often, however, fame is awarded for notable achievements of value to society; and because the fame motive has its origin in the need to belong and the desire for acceptance and approval, good works undertaken to become famous are not a surprise. A survey asked persons who had said in an earlier survey that they would like to be famous (30 percent from that survey), "If you had the talent to be the best at any one thing, what would you most like to be famous for?" The most chosen answer—from a list of twenty occupations, such as musician, athlete, artist, parent, and others—was "Doing good/Being good (humanitarian)."[2] This may be, in fact, the most reliable path to fame.

The desire for fame is one of the giant engines of human action. Nevertheless, throughout history, it has often been asserted that the pursuit of fame is immoral and bad for society. It can produce theft, deceit, lies, rumor, murder, war. It can waste talent on shoddy objectives. But is the fame motive any more damaging to society than the power motive or the money motive? It can inspire great, unselfish deeds that are clearly of social value. Where would we be without the inventor in the garage, the artist in the attic, the scientist in the laboratory, the explorer up the uncharted river? In the end, it's the outcome that counts.

Seeking fame through philanthropy is a rising trend. Wealthy people used to want to stay unknown, but now they want to be famous for their donations. Many of these are rich prizes given annually, with the donor's name attached to it.

It's also true that many who seek fame through actions honored by society may try again and again without succeeding. As essayist William Hazlitt wrote a century ago, "The way to fame through merit alone is the narrowest, the steepest, the longest, the hardest of all others."[3] Some will give up or set out on a less noble path—without (let us hope) resorting to strange or deviant acts—accepting failure like the poor who refuse to steal. In *The Temple of Fame,* Alexander Pope gives speech to such a one: "Unblemish'd let me live or die unknown. Oh, grant an honest fame, or grant me none!"[4]

Associates and Families

Many seek fame through reflected glory: association with famous people or institutions, perhaps a friend, partner, team member, employer, spouse, parent, or child. One can be born to fame because of lineage, such as royal descent, or through relation, such as the brothers of U.S. presidents Jimmy Carter and Bill Clinton. Then not only can you do nothing, but you can be nothing. One source observed about another man,

> In some cultures, you can use family pedigree, ethnicity, how educated your parents were. Then you have less of a need to be famous, because you can reassure yourself. In an autobiography, he says, "I was ten years old, I was doing poorly in school, I was homely, I was awkward, I couldn't play sports, and I was very anxious, and the way I reassured myself was to say to myself over and over again, 'How bad can I be, because my great-great-great-grandfather was John Adams?'" He says, "Wait a minute, I had great ancestors, I don't have to be famous myself."

Another interviewee gave a different example of borrowed fame:

> Sure, I wanted to be recognized, but I realized I was not going to be able to do it, so I took the route of joining an organization where I play an important role and I knew the organization would be famous—I could help make it famous, therefore, since I am a member of that famous organization. And when I am introduced to people, they say, "Oh, well, you're this," and therefore they recognize me and talk about me and say, "He belongs; he has an important job."

One may seek fame through protégés—helping another to become famous. Examples of this, I once wrote, include "trainers and athletes (the first textbook on training was written in Athens in 444 BC), teachers and students, masters and apprentices, parents and children (especially in immigrant families), patrons and artists, mentors and students, power brokers and public officials, clergy and kings, directors and actors, agents and show business people, sponsors and candidates, caddies and golfers, and perhaps even jockeys and horses."[5] In the 1981 film *Chariots of Fire,* when his charge wins the big race, the Italian coach of a young English runner says with pride, "I've waited thirty years for this."

A generation ago, two thirty-five-year-old professors competed for promotion to a choice tenured appointment. Some months after the selection was made, the loser committed suicide. A year later, the winner's mentor, the professor under whom he had obtained his PhD degree, said to me with pride, "You know what killed him? My boy killed him. He was too tough for him."

An unusual but increasingly frequent example of reflected glory is the connection between the staff and trustees of private foundations with the foundation's grant recipients. When the grantee is already famous or becomes famous, the foundation personnel can claim some of the recognition for themselves, as one interviewee acknowledged.

> Yes. You know the MacArthur Fellows program, of course. The socalled Genius Awards. That's like the definition of becoming famous.
>
> *And to be associated with that brings recognition.*
>
> Well, yeah. All of us here at the foundation certainly bask in the reflective glory of the Fellows program.

Another interviewee said,

> Well, the administrative people with the National Institutes of Health
> are usually people who don't do research and haven't done research for
> a long time. And many of them recognize they aren't going to be par-
> ticularly prominent in their research field. And they say, "Well, let's as-
> sociate with a successful program and be the administrator of that pro-
> gram and associate with the people who are going to be doing the
> things and get recognition that way." And those are the people I've
> dealt with at the institute for the last twenty-five years.

All of us are familiar with name-dropping: mentioning or proclaiming
that one knows a famous person. A national poll in 1987 asked, "Here is a
list of things. As I read down the list please tell me for each item whether
or not most people think of it as a symbol of achievement or status." For
the item "Knowing people who are prominent or famous," 63 percent of
respondents chose "Yes," 33 percent chose "No," and 4 percent chose
"Don't know." A related question with different wording was also asked:
"Here is a list of things. As I read down the list, please tell me for each item
whether or not you personally think of it as a symbol of achievement or
status." For the same item, "Knowing people who are prominent or famous," 38 percent of the respondents chose "Yes," 58 percent chose "No,"
and 3 percent chose "Don't know."[6] The respondents thought that other
people would be especially impressed by name-dropping but acknowledged that they, too, could be impressed.

"Successful systems accumulate parasites," writes Hugh Hixson in the
journal *Science*. In an article about the "top 20 great ideas of science," he
goes on to say, "This is a fundamental observation, rooted in the thermo-
dynamic observation that it is easier to move (or steal) something than it is
to make it."[7] In other words, it's much easier to name-drop than to make
a name for oneself. Through e-mail, however, one can do both. A young
girl directed a message to a long list of acquaintances, including one who
was famous. "I want to tell everyone I know this person," she explained.
This use of e-mail is not uncommon, since it ascribes importance to the
sender regardless of whether the connection with the famous recipient is
close, distant, or imaginary.

A woman who was a prospective juror in a bombing trial tried to get
seated on the jury. When the judge asked if her purpose was to "get famous
like the O. J. Simpson jury," she said yes.[8] You may drop the names of fa-

mous people. When John Kennedy Jr. established residence in New York City many people claimed to know him. Or, as one woman said, "I didn't know him, but my dog knew his dog.

One familiar path to fame is association with one's own family. A fame-motivated parent may try to become famous through a child's achievements, with the family's most promising child naturally the focus of parental ambition. The parent may want the child to become rich and/or powerful and, in many instances, certainly wants the child to become famous.

Stories of "stage mothers" are perhaps the most common examples of fame-motivated parents. One woman tried to hire a killer to murder her neighbor. Her purpose was to help her daughter win a cheerleading contest over her neighbor's daughter. She thought that by having the girl's mother killed, she would cause so much grief that the girl would not be a threat to her daughter in the next year's competition.[9] An HBO documentary describes a milder melodrama, children's southern beauty contests, particularly the participation of a very pretty five-year-old girl. Her mother concentrates on her to the exclusion of her three other children, and even though she is a waitress of modest means, she has spent tens of thousands of dollars to prepare her daughter for participation.[10] The following is from an interview with a twenty-year-old man who, after a successful period as an actor in his hometown, was studying for a career in musical comedy.

Do you know anyone who lived through the achievements, the fame, of someone else? Mothers with daughters in beauty contests are examples.

Mothers are the number one culprits as fame searchers, not for themselves, but for their kids. Definitely. I can't tell you the number of mothers who have put their kids in lessons from an incredibly young age and have been consistently doing this every step of the way. You know my mother can't stand them. It's incredibly pushy, and when you speak with them you see they want their kid to be famous. There's a musical about this.

Gypsy is about that, right?

Yes. It's a very famous show about this stage mother who is living vicariously through the child, pushing, pushing, pushing, until the kid leaves her and she is miserable. These people really exist.

So what happens when it's clear that the child is not going to make it?

To them?

To the child and to the parent.

It's hard because it really does take some people five, ten years to realize what's going to happen. Most people try to start performing around the age of twenty, but I say if nothing has come up, you know, by twenty-five, by that point the mother may have already given up; she really doesn't have any other choices. Probably the child is taking a little longer to give up.

So this has gone on from age five to twenty-five?

Could be. Yes.

Calls for Attention

Acts to gain attention have been with us long before the eating of snakes on current reality television. They have taken the form of tattoos, strange clothes, even drinking wine from human skulls (done by a group in Paris around 1830). "It's not right," says one person who speaks for many. "All the weirdos get attention, and the good people don't get noticed or recognized."

Sometimes the actions are directed to friends and other familiar groups, with the fame motive perhaps latent. These are the little episodes we see over and over in everyday life, such as a person who always speaks up in meetings but has nothing to say. They can begin at an early age. From seventh grade, I remember a boy at the margin of his peer group who hit on the idea of chewing garlic in class and then running up to his classmates in the corridors and blowing in their faces. He got attention all right.

When large audiences of strangers are involved, the fame motive becomes more obvious. Michael Portnoy, a performer, charged the stage at the Grammy Awards and broke into a wild dance with the words "Soy Bomb" painted on his chest. This act brought him enough recognition for him to declare, "My work on the Grammy introduced me to the public." He has since had offers to "soy bomb" other events.

In an article entitled "John Kerry Was YouTubed, Bro, for Show," journalist Fred Grimm describes an occasion at the University of Florida when the 2004 presidential candidate was speaking. A twenty-one-year-old man seeking national attention went to an open microphone and kept asking questions of Kerry. Finally, campus police moved in and arrested him. Meanwhile, a strategically located friend with a video camera had carefully recorded the entire confrontation for the public.[11]

Ivan Wilzig, a "millionaire hipster," liked to circulate through New York City nightlife wearing a cape and accompanied by his girlfriend. According to a contemporary account, "Sir Ivan and his cape inspire all manner of unsolicited commentary, some admiring, some disparaging . . . [H]e doesn't really mind, as long as people notice."[12]

As most of us have seen, alcohol will loosen one's restraint on attention-seeking behavior, just as it can for aggression and sexual behavior. Some people are notorious for their drunken attention-seeking actions: lampshades for hats at a cocktail party and so on. In karaoke bars, release from inner sanctions comes quickly. Any customer can use the microphone to sing and is usually allowed at least one complete solo. In an Ohio bar, three or four women who had been bridesmaids in a wedding showed up after the party in their long dresses. The band came over to sit with them and gave one a nickname, something like "Miss Florida." When they went back to play, she insisted on singing, though when she sang at church, people moved away from her in the pews because of her poor voice. At the bar, she climbed over the tabletops in her long dress to get to the stage.

It's a frequent complaint that genuine high achievers are too often overshadowed by mere celebrities. The word *celebrity* is derived from the Latin noun *celebritas,* meaning "fame and renown." Celebrity itself is "the condition of being much extolled or talked about; famousness, notoriety."[13] These days, though, "celebrity" has acquired a special meaning, designating someone who has become a public figure through planned and sought-after media exposure that injects his or her name and image into the popular culture. Since most such persons have done nothing that deserves to be publicly praised—merely being "famous for being famous"—their time in the limelight is usually brief. But there is no shortage of would-be successors in a media-saturated society, and there are plenty of ways for them to get noticed.

Joshua Gamson, a scholar who studies celebrity in modern culture, writes about the work of Daniel Boorstin,

> Boorstin argued that, with the growth of mass media, public relations, and electronic communication, it is possible to produce fame without any necessary relationship to outstanding action or achievement. Thus the hero, whose fame is the result of distinctive action or exceptional,

meritorious character, has been superseded by the celebrity, whose notoriety is manufactured by mass media without regard for character or
achievement.[14]

Gamson notes, in an article in the *International Encyclopedia of Social and
Behavioral Sciences,* that "celebrities are a distinctly contemporary form of
famous person and are the result of modern communications media which
make it possible to achieve notoriety without benefit of extraordinary action or achievement."[15]

Celebrities get help, as we all know, from publicity agents, public relations firms, gossip columnists, and how-to books on getting noticed.
David Giles writes,

> If celebrity is essentially a media production, rather than the worthy
> recognition of greatness, then its purest form must exist through the
> powers of hype. Hype in its truest sense must have no object of any
> value; of course, great writers and performers have never been averse to
> a spot of good publicity, but hype implies that a phenomenon can be
> made to appear valuable, even when its value is non-existent.[16]

The Internet has become a most useful media tool for people seeking
celebrity. One interviewee said,

> I particularly enjoyed just reading about the whole history of fame, dat-
> ing way back to the coin, and how it all developed and how it's changed
> with the introduction of new technology, and I was actually going to
> comment that I think it's going one step further with the introduction
> of the Web in that now it is in a way much easier to enter into the fray
> of becoming famous because of the Web. For example, my twelve-year-
> old son, David, was in a movie. He played a part, worked for just one
> day, yet you can find him on the World Wide Web, and you can find
> his credit through a data search, and it's allowed him to essentially be-
> come famous throughout the world even though he's not really. It's just
> opened up a whole new avenue for people to become famous or even
> to think that they're famous, knowing that their name is out there on
> the Web.

One way to call attention to oneself through the Internet is with a blog
in which the authors describe personal thoughts and events in their lives.

There was a time when people had to keep many things to themselves. But in a completely wired world, with barriers to communication more or less eliminated, this seems to have disappeared. To walk through the videos on YouTube, for example, is to visit with tens of thousands of people who are saying what amounts to "Look at me! Look at me!" and little more. Never in history have we had the opportunity to see and hear an extraordinarily large number of people who are driven by the fame motive. They don't care what they are famous for; they just want to be famous. They want an Internet hit rate that is off the charts.

Millions of people post these notices about themselves containing personal notes and photos. In addition to blogs we now have sites like MySpace, Facebook, and Twitter. These are directed to a worldwide audience of known and unknown people. Tens of millions of people are accessible this way, and more keep coming. In one instance, a woman writes, "Growing up, I was the fat girl . . . When the bottle landed on me during spin the bottle, the boys chanted, 'Do it over.'" She describes her experience in college where she was "the only woman in her class uninvited to join a sorority." In her blog, which has become very popular, with many international viewers, she writes about her personal life today.[17]

Another way to gain attention is to set some record of achievement in actions that are unimportant and sometimes deviant and strange. The *Guinness Book of Records* lists dozens of them—from the good to the evil, from the normal to the bizarre. This well-known annual compilation has become one of the world's largest-selling books and is a number one gatekeeper to fame, in part because it doesn't discriminate between socially valued achievements and those that aren't. Categories in the 2000 millennium edition are courage, knowledge, achievement, wealth, fame, media and pop culture, the body, technology, danger and disaster, and sports. Top billing in these categories goes to lifesavers, medical heroes, special skills, competitive eating and drinking, the superrich, sports stars, world leaders, criminals, country music stars, acts of transformation, body phenomena, accomplishments using computers (i.e., the biggest prime number found using a computer), environmental disasters, and track and field competitors.[18]

It's a strange mix. Most of the individuals cited by name have done something of social value, such as lifesavers, space heroes, epic adventurers, scientists, inventors, and so on. To have a separate section on fame seems odd, because so many of those whose names appear in the other sections are famous, but it turns out that this section is mainly devoted to stars of show business and sports. World leaders are also included, but less for their personal achievements than for oddities, such as the most expensive presidential inauguration, the most descendants to become prime minister, and so on. Record-setting criminals have their categories as well: most prolific murderers, biggest robberies, longest time on death row, and the like. In the sections on achievement and the body, we find records for bizarre actions to call attention to one's self. They include the longest pull of two railroad cars using teeth, the most weight lifted from one's ears, the most eggs balanced on end simultaneously by one person, the most pierced man, and the longest mustache (with a total span of eleven feet and eleven inches).

What are these people trying to do? Their goal is to know that they are unique, surely, but also to have their achievements recognized by others, to have their name seen by millions of people—even if only for a moment—and to have name and records carried forward into the future. One interviewee discussed a case in point.

> People do crazy outlandish things just to get attention . . . Something like Michael Jackson. I think he's such an interesting case with all his surgery he's had, and God knows what he's really like. But have you seen this recent news where he dangled his baby over the balcony?
>
> *I was watching the same show. He is most famous for his 1982 pop music album* Thriller, *which sold twenty-four million copies and broke all records for that time. But he said, "For the first time in my life, I feel I have achieved something; I'm in the* Guinness Book of Records."
>
> Isn't that incredible? So it isn't for the money he's doing all these things, really; it's for the notoriety, the fame. Wasn't he one of a large family and maybe felt that he was at the bottom. I don't know his life history—I mean, what he's gone through. I don't know who he's trying to look like. His poor face. You just can't imagine doing that to yourself. And all for, I guess, fame. Can't think of any other reason.

The purest case of getting your name before the public without doing anything at all is portrayed in the film *It Should Happen To You.*[19] The idea for the film came to writer Garson Kanin in a most unusual way.

> In 1952, Kanin's wife, actress and writer Ruth Gordon, was feeling very depressed. While out driving around New York City one day, Kanin entertained the notion of putting her name on an empty billboard as a

way to cheer her up . . . Although he opted not to go through with it he thought the idea would make a good story. As he elaborated on it he determined that the main character should be someone who was un-known, but desperately seeking to become famous.[20]

In the film, actress Judy Holliday plays the role of Gloria Glover, a young woman from upstate New York who says, "I came to [New York City] to make a name for myself." Gloria was a successful model at first but then gained weight and was fired from the agency. She says, "If I go back home now, no one will ever have heard of me." She had a thousand dollars saved, so as a solution to her problem, she rents a double-sized billboard on Columbus Circle and has her name painted on it in huge letters. She trades her spot on this highly desirable billboard for six other smaller billboards around Manhattan and has her name painted on these.

People begin talking about her, wondering who Gloria Glover is. Then, by chance, she becomes recognized while shopping in Macy's, the big de-partment store. A clerk is looking out the window at one of the billboards while Gloria signs her name to a charge. The clerk sees her name and lets out a little shriek, pointing at the billboard and saying, "Are you her?" A small crowd gathers, asking questions and seeking autographs. Subse-quently, Gloria is asked to participate in a talk show to tell her story and becomes known to a wider audience. Shortly after that, she is taken over by a publicity agent, under whose direction she becomes famous as the "all-American girl."

At the end of the story, we see Gloria at a military ceremony in which a big plane for the U.S. Air Force has been named after her. Her name is painted on the nose of the airplane. At this point, in the absence of public censure, Gloria turns on herself, saying, "Don't name it after me—there's no sense in it. It is wrong. The name should stand for something—not nothing."

Strange and Deviant Acts

The fourth path to fame I will discuss here is through an act that is injuri-ous—even evil—in the judgment of the general public but that brings ex-traordinary attention. Infamy, this type of fame, may be unsought, unin-tended, or unwanted by the actor, but there are many times when it is sought. How can this be? I propose two explanations.

The first explanation is that, surprisingly, the point has been reached where one would rather be infamous than have no response at all. A person says, "I don't care anymore what they think. At least they know I am here," or, "I don't care about your approval, but I'll make you remember me." The best-known legend of an infamous action involves Herostratus. He wanted to make his name live in history. He was a shepherd who burned down the Great Temple of Diana in 356 BC. This temple was started in 440 BC at Ephesus and was built in 120 years. It was considered one of the Seven Wonders of the Ancient World. The authorities at Ephesus, it is said, forbade the mention of Herostratus by word of mouth or in writing, under the penalty of death. Ironically, his name became well known despite this censure. He is now the symbol of infamy in the Western world. Miguel de Cervantes writes in *Don Quixote,*

> And something of the same sort is what happened in the case of the great emperor Charles V and a gentleman in Rome. The emperor was anxious to see that famous temple of the Rotunda, called in ancient times the temple "of all the gods," but now-a-days, by a better nomenclature, "of all the saints," which is the best preserved building of all those of pagan construction in Rome, and the one which best sustains the reputation of mighty works and magnificence of its founders. It is in the form of a half orange, of enormous dimensions, and well lighted, though no light penetrates it save that which is admitted by a window, or rather round skylight, at the top; and it was from this that the emperor examined the building. A Roman gentleman stood by his side and explained to him the skillful construction and ingenuity of the vast fabric and its wonderful architecture, and when they had left the skylight he said to the emperor, "A thousand times, your Sacred Majesty, the impulse came upon me to seize your Majesty in my arms and fling myself down from yonder skylight, so as to leave behind me in the world a name that would last forever." "I am thankful to you for not carrying such an evil thought into effect," said the emperor, "and I shall give you no opportunity in the future of again putting your loyalty to the test."[21]

The second and very different explanation for why people sometimes appear to seek infamy is that the act considered deviant and infamous by the main society truly does come from a desire for fame, not infamy. The same act can bring both fame and infamy because values differ in society. It is not always the general public that is the audience for the fame seeker.

For many, there is a special audience, not society at large, and for some, the quest for fame may be directed to audiences that have deviant values from the general public's point of view. The achievement that may bring fame from the deviant group may be viewed as an achievement of high value. Leaders of countercultural movements (e.g., feminism, marginalized sexual orientations, the Black Panthers or other radical groups, or even revolutions) are seeking fame among other countercultural groups in the United States and simply do not care—or, in fact, pride themselves—that the larger society views their actions as infamous.

As Goode writes, those who reject their social group's norms yet still have a desire for prestige will often seek it from a smaller, deviant group.

> A man may be widely admired in a slum area as a hustler who makes a good living by chicanery, fraud, and threat, but in other circles he may encounter abhorrence or contempt. In some art circles the work of Rauschenberg, Oldenburgh, and Warhol may be given respect, but in others it may be evaluated as vulgar and fraudulent. That is, the prestige given in one group may not be transferable over group boundaries.[22]

I quote again from *Don Quixote*.

> "That, Sancho," returned Don Quixote, "reminds me of what happened to a famous poet of our own day, who, having written a bitter satire against all the courtesan ladies, did not insert or name in it a certain lady of whom it was questionable whether she was one or not. She, seeing she was not in the list of the poet, asked him what he had seen in her that he did not include her in the number of the others, telling him he must add to his satire and put her in the new part, or else look out for the consequences. The poet did as she bade him, and left her without a shred of reputation, and she was satisfied by getting fame though it was infamy."[23]

Some deviant groups in the United States are made up of individuals often unknown to one another but alike in their disregard for the opinion of the larger society. Graffiti artists are contemporary examples.

In a descriptive analysis of their culture, Sutcliffe writes, "The most recognizable form of graffiti is called a tag . . . It's also the most prevalent because these short, two- to five-letter words can be written quickly, posing virtually no risk to the artist of being caught." A tag's simplistic style allows the writer to focus on quantity—a high priority for someone looking to get their name known around town. "Graffiti is not a random impulse," says Sutcliffe, "but rather a methodical act designed to call attention to the writer's existence. Fame is their most important goal." Sutcliffe concludes, "Writers know that to be recognized, people have to see their work, which is why they choose visible structures such as overpasses and buses to paint their illustrations. Style is also essential to achieving fame; graffiti artists know their work has be eye-catching to get the public's attention."[24]

Murderers, assassins, and serial killers must be noted here for the possibility that a desire for fame is the cause of their actions. After reviewing studies of such criminals, however, I've concluded that their motives are too varied for generalization. Among the assassins, some may be seeking current fame from a part of society that hates the target and would be glad to see him or her dead (e.g., the Wehrmacht officers who plotted to kill Hitler). They may be seeking posthumous fame, believing that the nation in later years will realize that it was saved from disgrace (e.g., John Wilkes Booth). For some, the fame motive may be transferred, with the murderer seeking to publicize a message or a belief or a cause, while remaining personally unknown (e.g., Ted Kaczynski, who acted anonymously as the Unabomber). The murderer may be mentally ill (e.g., Mark Chapman, who killed John Lennon). When declared "innocent of his crime by reason of insanity," John Hinckley, who stalked Jody Foster, was outraged, feeling that the judgment diminished him.[25]

Like graffiti artists, some criminals may simply want to assert their individuality, to say, "I was here!" The psychologist Jonathan Adler describes the musical *Assassins*.

> It's a musical whose characters are nine people who have tried, successfully or not, to assassinate the president of the United States . . . [T]he eight other assassins, led by John Wilkes Booth, converge upon Lee Harvey Oswald in the Texas Book Depository and convince him that killing [President] Kennedy will be the only way for him to "be someone" . . . I think the true theme of this show is that the worst possible thing for an American is to be forgotten—to not achieve some degree of recognition. And so these poor, desperate people resort to this unimaginable crime in an effort to be remembered. "People will hate me!" Oswald says to Booth, when he realizes what he is being asked to do. "They'll hate you with a passion!" Booth responds; "Imagine people

having passionate feelings about Lee Harvey Oswald!" Obscurity is the true fear.

Maureen Orth draws the same conclusion about a real-life assassin.

My own experience of death as the ultimate high dive into fame came when the obscure serial killer Andrew Cunanan shot Gianni Versace on the steps of the flamboyant designer's Miami mansion in 1997 . . . He knew very well that the act of murdering Versace would instantly cata-pult him to where he had long fantasized about being: at the center of worldwide attention . . . Wherever he went, he craved the limelight and aspired to the top, whether through charm or falsehood. In the end, he reached an exclusive pinnacle that provided him with the celebrity he had always sought: he became America's most-wanted fugitive.[26]

Among us are those who claim to be murderers. John M. Karr con-fessed to the 1996 JonBenet Ramsey killing. Clearly, he wanted to become infamous as a murderer, with his name in the news, and must have been disappointed when DNA tests refuted his claim. According to officials in Boulder, Colorado, before Karr showed up, two hundred others had al-ready confessed to the killing.

In regard to serial killers, infamy may or may not be the purpose. In a letter to the Wichita police, a serial killer complains, "How many times do I have to kill before I get my name in the paper or get some national at-tention?" Only with his sixth homicide, he said, had he begun to get any publicity. Enduring infamy goes to some serial killers, such as Jack the Ripper and the Boston Strangler, but was that their reason for their acts? After reviewing several studies on serial killers, author Joyce Carol Oates concludes that many of the killers keep silent about their acts.[27]

The preceding discussion leads me to three observations:

1. It's likely that an activity chosen to bring fame will be one that the fame seeker enjoys and aspires to succeed in for its own sake, an ef-fort that may be intrinsically rewarding even without fame. Actors and professional athletes offer obvious examples. (This may be hard to believe about some of the people in the *Guinness Book of Records*. Did the man with the eleven-foot mustache actually enjoy it?) Then, as life goes on, the rewards of the chosen path may fade away, and a new path to fame and occupational enjoyment may be sought. Ac-

tors appear in TV commercials and game shows; athletes become sports commentators and after-dinner speakers.

2. In seeking fame, some people—perhaps most—will try a number of approaches more or less concurrently. This program of trial and error was mentioned in an interview about a certain celebrity.

> He's a good person but I think he has to have some drive there to be known and famous.
>
> *To appear in so many different places?*
>
> Yes. Because you can say no. Somebody asks you to do something, you don't have to do it. You can be selective, and you can only say yes if you think there is something new and different and important. I don't think he does that. He's not selective in that way. He just takes whatever opportunity there is. I do think at some point people who get famous get a little bit selective, because they realize they don't have the time to do everything, and they are only going to pick things that they think will help them with their ticket to fame; but I think initially it may be just do everything and anything in quantity, not quality. I think that's the negative side of the fame motive, just get your name out there.

3. Over time, the actions people take in pursuit of gaining fame or keeping it are likely to change. Sometimes, the change is benign. For example, President Jimmy Carter, after being rejected by the American public, gave up politics and turned to seeking and attaining the Nobel Peace Prize. We may advance from simple celebrity to an action of value to society: for example, with photographers present, a movie star adopts a third-world child. In another example, the plutocrat Warren Buffet, perhaps tired of reading about how rich he is, announced that most of his fortune will go to a charitable foundation (founded by another plutocrat not indifferent to public attention, Bill Gates). The most likely change comes after trying for a notable and valued achievement and not succeeding. There is a shift to emphasizing associations with famous people, or creating a "look at me" personality style, with a repertoire of attention-getting acts; or one may even degrade into strange and deviant behavior, still mistakenly seeking the approval of the original audience.[28]

Summary

- There are four well-established routes to fame: (1) achievements of high value to society; (2) association with famous others; (3) acts taken only to bring attention to oneself; and (4) strange and deviant acts, often infamous.

- Few are able to become famous through achievements of high distinction, no matter how hard they may try.

- Many people who have acquired fame through actions of value to society will try to increase their fame by becoming celebrities rather than through further good works.

- What is done in pursuit or maintenance of fame is likely to change during life, as one tries to deal with failures.

7 ☆ Presentation of Self

Seven Kinds of Recognition

Marilyn Monroe's body became known long before she did. The hugely successful nude calendar she posed for prior to landing a movie contract did not mention her name. Fame arrived only later, as her name became known.

Without being known by name, one will rarely become famous. Often, nothing else is needed. Many authors, scientists, government officials, and the like are known only by their names. (What did Dr. Spock or Agatha Christie look like?) It is better, however, to be known for name and fame or name and voice together. For a beautiful woman, the face may come first; for a ranting politician, the voice. Without the quick follow-up of a name, however, recognition will quickly fade—as it did for Marilyn Monroe's body.

Ideally, one will be known for all three—name, face, and voice—and it is this full image that the fame seeker will strive to put before the public. A well-known 1959 study by Erving Goffman entitled *The Presentation of Self in Everyday Life* describes people's efforts to present themselves to others in ways that elicit favorable responses and confirmations of their own self-image.[1]

There was a time when humans didn't have names. In the most primitive form of recognition, individuals could discuss another person whom they identified by pointing, with a nod or some other gesture, or perhaps by reference to some physical characteristic or past action of the other. Once naming appeared in human culture—years ago—people could talk about another person if he or she were elsewhere. Through name identification, an individual could in effect "travel"—become known by word of mouth in the nearest settlement and beyond.

The next step was visual identification: portrait coins, statues, and, later, portrait painting made it possible to add an image to a famous name. Portrait medals of rulers appear in the earliest Etrusco-Roman history and were most fully developed in the Italian Renaissance. In *The Currency of Fame: Portrait Medals of the Renaissance,* editor Stephen K. Scher writes, "One of the most original and complete means of fulfilling the Renaissance desire for fame and immortality was the portrait medal, for within the confines of this small, durable, portable, and easily reproduced object was contained a wealth of information about the subject represented."[2] Coins and medals could not only spread awareness of a ruler's name but endow it with weight and importance as well. Statues and paintings that didn't travel were constant reminders to his subjects of their ruler's presence and importance.

None of this was available to the common folk, of course. For most people, face recognition did not exist apart from an individual's actual presence until the invention of photography in the nineteenth century (although a few newspapers would occasionally carry drawings of persons in the news). Within a few years of the 1839 invention of the daguerreotype, which made it possible to make photographic portraits of millions of people, photography had spawned a whole industry of image reproduction.

Finally, with the invention of sound recording, voice became a third element of recognition independent of a person's presence. Before television, fame of this kind was uncommon. Gabriel Heatter's distinctive voice was nationally famous for a fifteen-minute nightly newscast on radio, which he often began with a hearty, often-parodied, "Ah, there's good news tonight"; he never appeared himself. Marion and Jim Jordan, a husband-and-wife comedy team, appeared for years on radio as Fibber McGee and Molly. Their faces were unknown and remained that way, because their comedy style was too dependent on exaggeration to succeed in the more realistic medium of TV. Other successful radio comedians, notably Jack Benny, moved to television with success, but their faces were usually well known already from appearances in movies.

With conditions at last allowing one to become famous in name, face, and voice, fully seven kinds of recognition are now open to fame seekers. Recognition may come through all three conditions together, through one of three different combinations of the conditions in pairs (name and face, name and voice, face and voice), or through one of each of the three conditions alone. The combination of all three conditions was used to maximum effectiveness by political leaders Franklin D. Roosevelt, Winston Churchill, and Ronald Reagan. For prominent television personalities, the combination of name, face, and voice quickly loses its fame-producing power once they retire; Milton Berle, Arthur Godfrey, Chet Huntley, and Ed Sullivan, once known to almost every adult American, are now largely forgotten.

From today's perspective, the names, faces, and voices most likely to prove both lasting and vibrant are those of certain movie actors and actresses—Humphrey Bogart, Fred Astaire, John Wayne, Katherine Hepburn, Ingrid Bergman, and others—many of whose films of fifty years ago and more remain as entertaining as ever and, through television reruns and DVDs, have preserved the iconic luster of these great stars.

Name

If we had to choose between having a famous name without anyone knowing what we look like and having a famous face without anyone knowing our name—a nameless face or a faceless name—we would certainly choose the latter. To make a name for yourself, to be a household name, to see your name in lights—these are metaphors for the highest levels of individual achievement. A name can be known worldwide; it can endure over time; it also can assure one of a good table at a restaurant and of not being put on hold. Gloria Glover in the film *It Should Happen to You* (described in chapter 6) pays to have her name, not her face, painted on billboards throughout New York City. First things first.

Obviously, a name travels better, farther, and wider than a photograph or a voice recording. A name also is more durable, increasing one's chances of posthumous fame. Most important, in my view, is that one's name is the most accurate and complete label for one's sense of self. More than face, more than voice—both of which change over time—your name is who you are.

For fame seekers, to be known by name isn't all they want, but it's always what they want first and most. A Jamaican woman, a nurse who wants to be famous as a chef on television, commented on this wish in an interview.

One of the interesting things about wanting to be famous is whether people want to be famous for their name, their face, or both, or their voice only.

When you think about yourself on TV, I assume people will know your name and they'll know your face. If you—this is a strange question—if you did your show where you were nameless and the audience only saw your face and heard your voice but didn't know who you were, what would you say about that?

Well, I'd like to be known as the person who cooked that recipe that I am making, who, like the ads—"Who made that? What is the name of that person? Who did that? That's the best sauce I ever had. Who cooked the soup? The best soup I ever had. What's her name? I saw her on television, but I didn't know her name. I saw her face, but I didn't know who it was." So that's what I want them to remember.

The following is from another interview.

Some people may have famous faces but we don't know their names.

But I can't think of any. We don't know the name so that's not exactly fame is it?

Why not?

Well it's fame, yes, but it's not identifiable.

Why are you not famous unless your name is known?

Cause it never would reflect on you if only your face is known. You're getting no feedback. Then it's no good. But still, it's something, isn't it, better than nothing if you want to be famous, I suppose.

One's name may become famous to one's detriment. The following is from a conversation about presidents, actors, and fictional characters.

What about people who have a famous name? There are probably half a dozen Richard Nixons in the world that aren't Richard Nixon. How does that affect them I wonder. What if you were named Gomer Pyle, or your name was Art Carney, or something, and you weren't "the" Art Carney—how would that make you feel when, you know, you got made fun of?

A friend reports, "My sister has a friend named Harry Potter—what a change his life has seen."

Face

In adding a second characteristic to a famous name, face takes precedence over voice. Today, with photography now universal and requiring no special knowledge or skill, a connection between name and face is a simple matter to establish and reinforce. This, in turn, has led to an enormous increase in what might be called "commercial face." Every branded consumer product wants, above all, to have its name respected and remembered. Early branded products were given names implying quality (e.g., Acme, Gold Star, Sunkist), while founders' names expressed pride and implied reliability (e.g., Ford, Heinz, Campbell's, Hershey, Coors). The next step was to give a product an attractive visual identity via a made-up personality rendered in artwork (e.g., Betty Crocker, Aunt Jemima, the Quaker Oats Man, Old Grand-Dad). The appeal of imaginary faces to consumers led advertisers to use genuine ones (e.g., Frank Perdue of chicken fame, Orville Redenbacher of popcorn fame, and Leona Helmsley of hotel fame). Real people not only convey trustworthiness but can also appear in commercials for their own products.

Faces bring a story to life. Commercials for the American Express card cash in on this; along with the slogan, "You know my name, but not my face," they show pollster George Gallup and soccer star Pelé. Publishers, too, know the value of faces; the dust jacket of most books will display a picture of the author. The mid-nineteenth-century craze for *cartes de visite,* postcard-size photographs of the famous, reflected a deep-seated wish to put faces to famous names now that photography had made it possible. The proliferation of illustrated magazines soon followed. Today, photographers who hound celebrities are so numerous that they've acquired their own name, *paparazzi.*

Of course, not everyone with the fame motive wants face recognition by the public. Humorist Fred Allen once defined a celebrity as "a person who works hard all his life to become known, then wears dark glasses to avoid being recognized."[3] A facial disfigurement or declining beauty may be the reason. As she grew older, Marlene Dietrich refused to be photographed or even interviewed. Some celebrities may not want to be recognized in public places because of the danger of assault from a hostile crowd, even abduction. Perhaps the ideal kind of fame would be to have your name known and admired yet be able to walk the streets unnoticed. A writer can do that; a television personality cannot. Those whose work requires their faces to be public—athletes, for example—will try to avoid being accosted by their fans in airports and hotel lobbies by wearing dark glasses on even the gloomiest days.

Face fame without name fame—what would it be like? Because early films carried no credits, faces familiar to moviegoers remained anonymous at first. Around 1910, the adored actress Florence Lawrence was the first to be billed under her own name. Name billing steadily increased from then on and soon became standard for all roles of consequence.

In the case of star actors and actresses, the value of combining face and name is obvious. Character actors and bit players have benefited less, because moviegoers and television viewers can't easily connect a face they may have seen fleetingly many times with a name flashed on the screen fleetingly, along with others, at the beginning of a show. It's not unusual for strangers to ask quite veteran performers, "Don't I know you from somewhere?" or to remark after requesting an autograph, "Oh, is that who you are? I never heard of you." I discussed face fame without name fame in an interview with the editor of a magazine with over a million circulation.

You ran the column you wrote, along with your picture, on the back page of the magazine, and you said, "Well, 25 percent of magazine readers start at the back of the magazine." And then you said you were picking up something at your local newsstand and the proprietor there looked at you and said, "Don't I know you? Do you tend bar around here?"

Yeah, I'd forgotten that. And also in a bus station one time, when I had a television show on PBS that went for four years, a guy came up to me and said, "I know you." And I said, "Could I have your autograph?" And I felt like I was a subliminal celebrity, such that nobody, except for this guy, ever remembered my name. I looked like somebody familiar, somebody's brother.

So you would see people recognize your face but they didn't know who you were—didn't know your name. Did this bother you?

Sure, of course.

In 1974, I had an experience at a Frank Sinatra concert at Madison Square Garden. My daughter then worked for the television network broadcasting the show and offered me two tickets in the second row. She promised to have the camera point at me from time to time so I would be on national television. I figured that some of my friends would recognize me and get a kick out of it, as would I. So I went with my wife, wearing dark glasses—to look cool, I thought, on television.

The stage turned out to be a boxing ring in the center of the Garden, and our seats were between Joe Louis and friend on the left and Rex Harrison and friend on the right. Joe Louis, no longer the world's heavyweight champion but still famous, was already seated when Rex Harrison, then nearing the end of his acting career but also still famous, arrived and was seated. Louis, looking directly ahead and not turning, said, "Hello Rex," and Harrison, also looking straight ahead without turning, said, "Hello Joe." Several times during the concert, Frank Sinatra looked down from the stage directly at us, nodding to Joe Louis and Rex Harrison and peering at me in my dark glasses, clearly trying to figure out who I was.

Later, I saw my daughter and asked, "How did it go? How was I?" and she said, "We couldn't put the camera on you. It was your dark glasses that reflected the light. They made such a glare that the camera had to turn away. All we could show was your knee tapping to his singing."

After this, I felt stupid, ashamed. I thought, "What am I trying to do here to get my face shown." I had thought there might be a hundred people watching who would recognize me. And millions were watching who did not know me but might be curious for a moment. What kind of pathetic wish is it where I feel good by thinking that ten million people saw my face for a few minutes? In the end, I failed even at this. Instead, ten million people only saw my knee tapping.

Several years ago, a news release on some studies of human development that I had been conducting with colleagues was picked up by the *New York Times*. It appeared on the newspaper's Web site in the early morning hours, and by 6:30 a.m., NBC, CBS, and ABC had all called me to schedule interviews. Before noon, each had dispatched a camera crew to film me at home for that day's evening news broadcast. I watched myself on NBC and later learned that the caption "Oliver Smith" appeared on the screen on ABC as I spoke. (The other two networks got my name right.) Somehow, ABC had lost my name, but apart from thinking that they could at least have used more imagination (calling me, perhaps, Oliver Cromwell or Oliver Twist), it didn't bother me much. Name recognition would have been better, but face recognition was enough.

For a few people, face recognition may be welcome and even qualitatively appraised, while name fame is entirely unsought. This is true of the respondent in the following interview excerpt.

Last October, 2000, there was an international day of protest to stop the militarization of space in my hometown I joined a small group which met for a demonstration in front of the building on Main Street. Candid photos were taken and, along with a written report, were added to those from other cities throughout the U.S. and put on the Web site. To my stunned surprise, when I logged on, I found my photo holding a "Stop War in Space" sign staring at me from the computer. Then, in February, the head of the organization that had sponsored the day of protest came to town to speak and brought with him some of the thousands of postcards which had been printed with my photo on one side and, on the other, an appeal addressed to President Bush.

Well, I'm thinking about your face on thousands of postcards.

Oh yeah. Oh, by the way, did I tell you I made the *Nation* magazine?

And your face is on the Nation *now?*

Oh yes.

But it's an anonymous face so . . .

That's right.

I'm asking how you feel about your face being seen by . . .

I'm just glad it's a decent photograph.

. . . by tens of thousands of people who don't know who you are, and you're glad it's a decent photograph?

It's fun.

Do you wish they knew your name?

No. No, I'm just glad to be associated with the sign, and it's fun to be a totally unintentional, unintended part of the protest that I think is so import for us to preserve life on earth. No, I have no wish to have a name on it. Honest. It wouldn't mean anything anyway. I mean, I have maybe forty people who might recognize me, and that's it.

So putting a name on it wouldn't have made much difference, except people would know your name. Do you have any feelings about your face now being in so many places?

No, I'm just glad it's a nice-looking face. I mean, I have lots of pictures that are ugly. And I'm just relieved that it looks okay. You know. I don't need to be ashamed of the picture. That would bother me. Like the woman next to me in the postcard with her eyes closed. She's got her face all squeezed up. She's a very prominent, wonderful activist, and she looks terrible. I mean, you know, if I were to look like that and the postcard went out, I would be upset, yes.

Even though you're anonymous, you want your face to look right.

Yes. I want to be proud. I'm proud of being associated with this. I don't look as good as that most of the time, and I'm pleased that he chose that. He chose it for the sign, mostly, as much as my face, but he said, "You're dignified and determined," and those were the two things he wanted.

Voice

It's a huge void not to know what famous people of the nineteenth century and earlier sounded like—such people as Washington, Lincoln, Napoleon, Shakespeare, and Columbus. Now, thanks to his own invention, we know what Edison sounded like, not to mention the high-pitched voice of Theodore Roosevelt and the glowing tenor of Caruso.

As sound was coming to motion pictures, Harry Warner, one of the three brothers who founded the Warner Bros. studio, is said to have complained, "Who the hell wants to hear actors talk?" (He seems to have forgotten about the existence of theater.) Yet it was his company that took the risk of making the first film with sound, *The Jazz Singer* with Al Jolson. It started a revolution. Within two years, nearly all films made in Hollywood and elsewhere were made in sound.

The first to lose out were stars with heavy, non-English accents, such as Vilma Banky from Hungary, Pola Negri from Poland, and Emil Jannings from Germany. Once Hollywood's top leading man, John Gilbert proved to have a voice inappropriately high and saw his career quickly fade, although alcohol and general unreliability were also factors in his downfall. In 1933, Greta Garbo, who once had come close to marrying Gilbert and whose voice and slight Swedish accent had made the transition to sound with great success, arranged for Gilbert to have another chance, as her leading man in *Queen Christina*. The attempted comeback failed; he died three years later.

The advent of the "talkies," as they were first called, and their effects on

Hollywood were dramatized first in a brilliant stage comedy, *Once in a Lifetime* (1930), and later in an equally brilliant motion picture, *Singin' in the Rain* (1952). In the latter, a movie queen with a low-class accent and a crowlike voice saves her career when her voice is dubbed on the soundtrack of her first talkie by the film's golden-voiced heroine. Later, in front of a large audience, the deception is revealed, and all ends happily. Dubbing continued and still goes on, however. In the movie version of *My Fair Lady*, Audrey Hepburn lip-synched her songs while they were being sung by Marnie Nixon.

The public doesn't seem to mind this. When famous athletes like Michael Jordan and Tiger Woods appear in television commercials, they rarely speak but simply lend their presences to assure a hearing for a selling message from an unnamed voice. For the owners of such voices, anonymity is much preferred. When both face and voice are identified with a product, they are likely to be vetoed for other products. (The grocer who begged his customers, "Please don't squeeze the Charmin!" would inevitably remind viewers of that product even when promoting, say, a headache remedy or soap.) By keeping their fame unknown to the public, dozens of announcers with adaptable voices make good livings from recording voice-overs for TV commercials and public service announcements ranging from the cuddly to the commanding. Millions of times a day, every time an e-mail arrives for a client of America Online, a voice says, "You've got mail." Familiar and faceless, yes. But famous? No.

A recent book entitled *The Magic Behind the Voices: A Who's Who of Cartoon Voice Actors* is an earnest attempt to bring the profession more respect by profiling forty of the biggest names in that business.[4] This subject came up in my interview with a man in the film industry.

When I wanted to find out the name of the guy that does the voice of Elmo, I did a Web search and found a site that actually is all about people who work in the film and television industry. They're voice people. It's called VoiceChasers.org, and it's a fascinating site. You can look up about five hundred different people who, if you click on their name, it'll tell you all the voices that they've done. And you can also look at every animated or every puppet-related show that's ever been made. Type, click on it, and you can find out who the voice of, you know, Roger Rabbit or Daffy Duck or anything is. And it's remarkable how many voices Mel Blanc did. He was Daffy Duck, Bugs Bunny,

Porky Pig, Pepé le Pew, Wiley Coyote, Mr. Spacely on the Jetsons, Yosemite Sam, Tweety, Silvester, just to name a few. And he helped create the characters.

We didn't know who he was for a long time, right?

Mel Blanc? Yeah, I don't think people ever were interested in knowing who he was, but he did ultimately become a famous name. But very few people could recognize his face.

Sometimes people who are already famous—their picture, their name, everything is already famous—go into this voice work. Examples being Robin Williams, who's the voice of Aladdin in the animated movie of Aladdin; Jerry Orbach, who was on the TV show *Law and Order,* was the voice of Lumiere on *Beauty and the Beast;* Eddie Murphy, who's the famous comedy actor, plays the donkey in Shrek; Mike Meyers, also a famous comic actor, plays Shrek; James Earl Jones, who is a famous actor in his own right, is the voice of MCI commercials and the voice of MCI when you contact them on the telephone. People that are already famous have gotten into this area where they're making movies where their picture's not up there. Only voice.

Do they use their own voice, though?

You can definitely tell it's them. And they're hired because you can tell it's them. You hear the voice and you recognize it. You might not necessarily put two and two together that it is who it is, but if somebody said, "You know that's, by the way, Eddie Murphy," and then you go, "Oh, right, of course."

Although a famous voice frequently has no connection with a famous name or face, it becomes most memorable when embedded with the other two in a complete persona. Television newscaster Walter Cronkite is a casebook example. During the 1949–89 cold war, when hostilities with the Soviet Union seemed at all times possible and likely more than once, the U.S. government planned to have Cronkite be the announcer for all emergency radio broadcasts. In addition to his standing as a familiar and trusted national figure, Cronkite's voice was so well known that it alone was expected to certify the authenticity of the government's message.

Summary

- Three characteristics of a person—name, face, and voice—can be famous, either separately or in combination.
- The fame seeker's preference is to have all three, a complete presentation of self.
- The order of preference goes from name, to face, to voice fame.

8 ☆ Creating the Audiences

The Great Other Place

In the prehistoric culture of hunters and gatherers, who lived in isolated groups where everyone knew each other, the idea of fame could not arise. One might stand out among one's peers, but cave painters and petroglyph artists had no vision of their work being recognized beyond the tribe, by persons unknown. During the Middle Ages, the average peasant probably saw no more than one or two hundred other people in a lifetime, while at the upper reaches of society, distinction was earned or conferred through occupation or rank (e.g., the priesthood or the nobility) rather than individual accomplishment. In the fifteenth century, this began to change, through exploration and discovery, through the rebirth of the arts and literature, and (perhaps above all) by the invention and spread of printing. An educated and critically minded elite came into being, and gradually, with rising urbanization and the spread of newspapers, there was an ever more aware and informed set of publics around the world, each with its own culture but influenced by the cultures of others. Along with this came photography, then motion pictures, radio, television, and the Internet.

Today, instead of several hundred faces in a lifetime, we can see a thousand faces in a news broadcast. Audiences now are worldwide and unprecedentedly varied; more than twenty different languages have more than thirty million speakers. Richard Schickel, an eminent film critic, writes,

If you are born and raised in the boondocks and have the slightest sense of ambition, one fact becomes clear as soon as you become aware that the world is wide: that out there, away from your little bend on Moon River, people are doing interesting things, having more fun, and, in the end, accomplishing things that one cannot undertake locally. In the United States achievement obviously has several venues—New York, Los Angeles, Washington, for certain, and out beyond them the other world capitals of art, entertainment, thought, politics. In due course all these places tend to merge into a single country of the mind, "The Great Other Place," as I came eventually to think of it.[1]

In my experience, that "Great Other Place" fills the imagination before the child or teenager has any clear idea of its size and infinite variety. Once, while I was sitting with a granddaughter at twilight on a high floor of a condominium in Florida, we were watching the lights of Miami Beach as airplanes from all over the world arrived and departed, while freighters and cruise ships headed for the horizon en route to the Caribbean or South America or Africa. "There are so many places in the world," said the child in wonderment.

Without being at all clear on what's really out there, except that a lot is going on, young people can be determined to become part of it and to make a name for themselves. Theodore Dreiser describes such determination in his character Sister Carrie, when she is on her way to Chicago at age eighteen.

> Her hands were almost ineffectual. The feet, though small, were set flatly. And yet she was interested in her charms, quick to understand the keener pleasures of life, ambitious to gain in material things. A half-equipped little knight she was, venturing to reconnoiter the mysterious city and dreaming wild dreams of some vague, far-off supremacy, which should make it pray—the proper penitent, groveling at a woman's slipper.[2]

In 1942, at the age of nineteen, I left home and college to enlist and ended up as a B-24 pilot in the South Pacific. As I was saying my farewells, my twenty-four-year-old sister, an aspiring playwright whose interest in making a career in writing I shared, said, "And if you don't come back, I'll get there for you." We didn't need to discuss where or what "there" was, because it was the same to both of us: a wonderful, indefinable destination—a "Great Other Place"—that someday, somehow we would surely reach. We shared the fame motive in its simplest form: vague and unspecific, with often foolish dreams.

Small and Special Groups

For most fame seekers, the fame motive is directed toward small groups of people unknown to them. At the outset, they can range in size from one person, to several, to many, but the goal will always be to make the audience larger. The obvious way to do this is to appeal to groups beyond the original. Eminence in local boating, bowling, or golf circles may lead to eminence in community or business leadership, which in turn may result in articles (perhaps with photographs) in the local newspaper, receiving an award at a charity banquet, and so on. The fame may start specific and small but be additive over time (although I believe that most fame seekers would much prefer immediate and widespread recognition for a single achievement).

One man described his special audience in an interview.

> I happen to be famous within the world of youth baseball in my hometown. I'm not famous in any other dimension of my life. But I get enormous pleasure out of being famous in that one tiny little dimension, and it's because of, you know, commitment and enthusiasm and sort of an unflagging cheerfulness about the idea about helping young kids play baseball.

The following is from another interview.

And so, do you ever think of yourself as famous?

No. Well, I think I am "well known" by some subset of people. I think some of the things I have done are known by people, and so there is some recognition. There is some feeling of pride that some of my accomplishments are known and I get the credit. Fame would be, I think, a step up.

Or a step out?

Whatever. It's a little wider audience is the way I would put it. It's like when you said, "Fame means the people you don't know know of you," right? And certainly I would never find myself sitting next to a person on an airplane who wasn't a social scientist who said, "Oh my God, you're . . ." That could never happen to me.

The specialized audiences most likely to confer fame are found in and around one's occupation: lawyers, authors, scientists, businesspeople, for achievements great and sometimes small, are subject to lionization by their own kind. The *New York Times,* in announcing the MacArthur Foundation's "Genius Awards" of five hundred thousand dollars are well known to the public, but the winners of the awards are not. They are famous in their special sphere of achievement, but not in the world at large.

A famous athlete can be known only to sports fans, or a famous groundbreaking painter or sculptor can be unrecognized beyond the art world's avant-garde. One scientist describes fame in the field of physics as follows:

Einstein, Newton, Copernicus . . . are among the names that are best known outside of the science community, [but] much smaller achievements also often result in immortalizing individuals: the Yang-Mills theorem; the Chandrasekhar limit; the Josephson effect; the Richardson number; the Thomson coefficient; the Geiger counter; Faraday rotation; the Debye-Hückel theory; the Wheatstone bridge; the Weber-Fechner law. Such people (and their technical accomplishments) may be recognizable only to fellow scientists.[3]

Life circumstances occurring as early as high school or college can influence a choice of audience. When I was an undergraduate at Yale, there were nearly a thousand members of my class, of whom I might have come to know fifty or so in the year and a half before most of us left college to serve in World War II. In those days, the undergraduate body at Yale was dominated by students from New England prep schools who had formed friendships there and who arrived at Yale already members of a social group with established customs of dress, language, and manners. My very different background made me something of a misfit. I could walk the campus, under the elms, and only occasionally encounter someone I could greet and be greeted back by name. Needless to say, my classmates and others at Yale were not an audience to whom I aspired to be famous. In my self-image, I would be recognized by a large shadowy group—nameless except for Scott Fitzgerald and a couple of others.

In the years that followed, I hardly ever thought about my Yale class-mates, even though I did stay friends with four or five of them. It wasn't until the celebration volume for our fiftieth reunion was being prepared, when I was one of ten in the class who were invited to write a personal essay, that I realized I was a Yale graduate of some distinction even though I had never thought about it. At that time, another of the ten, who evidently was motivated by fame, said to me about a third member of the ten, "He's more famous than either of us." I realized that he had been thinking about his fame among our classmates and had kept track—for more than fifty years—of many of their careers, including mine, to appraise who was the most famous. In an interview, another classmate said, "Being well-known at Yale, being a famous graduate of Yale—that's pretty hot stuff. I think there are those who really work at being famous graduates of Yale."

To what degree do fame seekers define and choose their audiences? While fame on a large scale is almost always welcome, the audience whose opinion is most important to a fame seeker can be relatively small. Alvin Toffler, author of *Future Shock,* said to me at the height of his international fame, "What I really want to know is what the professors at Yale are saying." Braudy writes about Dante,

> Dante died in Ravenna after almost 20 years of political exile from Florence, still hoping he would be asked to return. The celebrity that he had already achieved in the rest of the world was not as important to him as acceptance by his native city. When the Laurel Wreath of Civic Poetry was offered to him by the University of Bologna two years before his death, he refused, because it could not be conferred on him in the Florentine church where he had been baptized.[4]

Just as those not yet famous can look forward in anticipation of an audience to be, so some already famous can look backward with regret at an audience that never was. Literary critic Clifton Fadiman said that he was living in the wrong century: the twentieth instead of the latter part of the nineteenth. My Yale history professor Frank Baumer wished he had lived in the Age of Enlightenment. They meant this, feeling that their beliefs, achievements, and standards were no longer valued as in earlier times and that the groups whose opinions and style of life they would have found ideal were gone from the human scene. This allowed them to reject much of the contemporary world and live as much as possible as they would have lived then.

One need not try to live in the past but can simply turn to the past. In his study of poets and their reference groups Robert Wilson says that one asserted with confidence, "If Shelley were alive today he would appreciate my work." The aging actor in the play *The Dresser* believes that he is discharging a responsibility to Shakespeare by continuing to fill the void left by young actors off at war. He is certain that Shakespeare would have approved.

People will seek fame from persons or groups who share their interests in life: a singer with the fame motive will seek out music lovers in hope of being recognized by people he or she respects for doing something he or she enjoys. But it also happens that a person hungering for fame can unsuspectingly drift into an audience where fame lies waiting. This sometimes happens to collectors. Most collections start innocently—as with a child's collection of butterflies or coins or stamps—and in time dies out as the collector loses interest. But if the interest is intrinsic and the collector is serious, determined, and able to keep adding to the collection, he or she will, in time, start comparing it to other collections of the same thing.

Among the many sections in the *Guinness Book of Records* is one on collectors and collecting. For collectors to be listed, however, there must be recognized competition in their respective fields. These can be large—there are millions of stamp collectors—or so small as to include only a dozen serious collectors. Whether the competition is large or small, the winners will be listed and thereby become famous to their fellow devotees.

One evening in 1965, on the commuter train from New York City to Old Greenwich, Connecticut, where I lived, the man sitting next to me opened his briefcase, took out a plastic bag of sand, and began to examine it. I was curious enough to ask him what it was. "It's beach sand," he replied, "I collect sand." So began a long friendship. Like almost everyone, I love ocean beaches. I think they were imprinted on me at an early age. In 1936 and 1938, I lived in Hawaii on Waikiki Beach, in a cottage close to the Moana and Royal Hawaiian hotels. Not being in school, I would spend the day on the beach. For fifty cents, I could rent a surfboard and buy a hamburger and a milkshake for lunch. These are precious childhood memories.

I told my new acquaintance of my interest in beaches, and he said he was forming a new club, the International Sand Collectors Society, devoted to collecting specimens of sand from beaches all over the world. He had some membership cards in his briefcase and signed me up before we reached our stop. I believe I was one of his first recruits. We turned out to be neighbors in Old Greenwich, and he got me started on my collection by giving me half a dozen sands from his surplus. Once I started my collection, we would often meet and exchange specimens.

During the sixty years that my wife and I were together, we traveled the world. We spent months on Caribbean islands, such as Grenada and Anguilla, before they were discovered by tourists. We ran together at dawn or twilight on one hundred of the world's great ocean beaches. With sand that we collected, but mainly with contributions from friends who traveled, my collection grew to sands from 950 different ocean beaches in more than 130 countries. My particular pleasure was in this diversity and in imagining the beauty of beaches where we had not been.

When we moved from New England to Florida, I donated my collection to the Harbor Branch Oceanographic Institution in Fort Pierce. Harbor Branch is the third largest oceanographic institution in the United States (the other two are Scripps Institution of Oceanography and Woods Hole Oceanographic Institution). Currently, the collection is stored in a large concrete bunker (for hurricane protection), along with HBOI's other collection of marine life, including what I believe is the world's largest collection of shells. Harbor Branch hopes to eventually build a museum in which all of them can be properly displayed. Meanwhile, the original International Sand Collectors Society was reorganized into something much larger, with hundreds of members. To many of them, the size and variety of my collection and the gift of it to HBOI came to stand as something of a model. There now were hundreds of people I didn't know but who knew of me. To an audience I had never sought or even thought of, I had become famous.

As I study people struggling to be famous, I see some who do not have an audience in mind: they have no image of themselves as famous to a specific public. They know what they want but not where to seek it. Role models can help one to focus, and famous people in show business often serve this purpose because they're so immediately visible to the budding fame seeker. Star athletes are visible, too, of course, but the great skills they possess can be intimidating, while lawyers, doctors, merchants, ministers, professors, and so on often aren't visible at all. A friend said, "Now, I knew a guy who wanted to be a singer, and that was strictly because he had seen this real singer, and this was the only model he had in his head, so he wanted to be a famous club singer."

Often, the choice of a role model goes wrong and leads a person to seek fame in an audience where the required achievements are of little interest to the person. Further, perhaps what is required—for example, the voice needed to be a famous club singer—is not among the person's talents. He or she might have climbed another mountain but got started up the wrong one. It is a sad case if the person tries to become famous by achievements that are of no interest personally and perhaps even repellent. Moreover, it may be a fame seeker may not even like the people in the audience—the people who are noticing and talking about him or her and making him or her famous. The fame seeker may be famous in this group, but that does not mean that he or she must like the people.

Actually, we do not need to search for or create small and special audiences for our fame motive. Increased social diversity in societies of all kinds and continuous exchanges among nations create more opportunities for those with the fame motive to reach particular audiences—although these, being specialized, are likely to be small. Halls of Fame are examples. There are Halls of Fame for checker players, cowboys, firemen, marble shooters, clowns, turkey hunters, dog mushers, exotic dancers, pickle packers. Of course, those honored in a Hall of Fame are there because of achievements that most of them regarded as an end in itself, not a path to fame.

The first Hall of Fame was established in 1900 by Henry Mitchell McCracken, then chancellor of New York University. His purpose was to create a site where only the most eminent Americans could be enshrined, to counteract the egalitarianism of the country's founding fathers. The irony is that McCracken's elitist concept of fame opened the door to its being broadened—some would say degraded—into an egalitarian concept that he would have hated. Since his time, Halls of Fame have proliferated, commemorating everything from baseball and rock and roll to special interest groups—an industry, an occupation, even a hobby. Great achievements of lasting value no longer are required. McCracken's original Hall of Fame, a collection of busts in a formal outdoor setting, is badly in need of upkeep, while active constituencies enable dozens of smaller ones to flourish. Humorists observe that with enough Halls of Fame, we can all become immortal.[5]

Always Wanting More

Surveys have shown us that most people don't care about being famous—probably because they're content with recognition from the small groups where they are known and whose judgment they value. For about ten years, I directed an international research group of twenty or so scholars from Europe and the United States who were leaders in the study of human development through the life span. We would meet several times a year, in places like London, Munich, New York, and San Francisco, to discuss our work and decide what should be done next to advance our area of research. Most of the twenty were content with each other's respect, but a few, motivated by fame, wanted a larger audience, of a size known only to them individually. It may have been four hundred scholars outside our circle but in the same line of work. It may have been four thousand fellow psychologists, forty thousand readers of *Science*, four hundred thousand readers of *Harper's*, a million readers of the *New York Times*, four million television viewers in the United States, or the four hundred million all over the world who watched the astronomer Carl Sagan on his television shows. My colleagues never said, but they surely dreamed.

Obviously, there are many different levels or degrees of fame. Examples of proper usage in Noah Webster's 1828 dictionary frequently refer to George Washington. Defining the word *summit* as "the highest point or degree, the utmost elevation," he adds, as an illustration, "The general arrived to the *summit* of human fame." Defining *diffuse* as "to send out or extend in all directions; to disperse," Webster offers two examples of usage: "Flowers *diffuse* their odors" and "The fame of Washington is *diffused* over Europe."

To illustrate, in a small way, how heights of fame may vary, I offer the dust jacket of my book *Ambition*. It included two levels of endorsements from seven or eight individuals. To the statements of Alvin Toffler and Betty Freidan, nothing was added but their names. The names of the other endorsers were followed by an identification, as in "Jonathan Piel, Publisher, *Scientific American*." A friend commented, "When I grow up I want to be like Toffler and Friedan."

U.S. postage stamps often carry a person's likeness: sometimes only a face; sometimes a face with a name; sometimes a face, a name, and an identification of some kind. As an example of the last, the Jonas Salk stamp carried both the face and name of the creator of the Salk vaccine and the identification "Medical Scientist." The *New York Times* makes fame-related distinctions among contributors to its op-ed page through its use of indefinite or definite articles in describing them: so-and-so is "a professor of history at New York University," or so-and-so is "an actress"; but W. H. Auden is "the poet," or Warren Buffett is "the investor and philanthropist."

In chapter 5, I cited *Time* magazine's seventy-fifth birthday gathering, which included persons who had appeared on one of the publication's weekly covers, as a concurrence of fame and infamy. Over the years, approximately five dozen persons have been named by *Time* as "Person of the Year," certainly an even more notable recognition. At the summit of fame might be the 250 individuals selected as "world famous" by Clive James for his 1993 book and television documentary series *Fame in the 20th Century.* James provides a glimpse of the selection process.

> It took a dozen of us almost all of the first week to agree on the 250 twentieth-century people who were genuinely, undeniably world-famous. Placido Domingo was out because his name was known only to everyone on Earth who liked the sound of good singing. Luciano Pavarotti was known even to people who couldn't tell good singing from bad, so he was in. Picasso was in and Matisse was out. Stefan Edberg was out because you had to be interested in tennis. John McEnroe was in because everybody was interested in bad behaviour. Those who were in got a blue card each so they could be pinned to the wall. It was incredible, the magnitude of some of the names that didn't get on that wall. When I realized that Margaret Mitchell was going to rate a mention but T. S. Eliot wasn't I argued for a pink card category for people who should get a *fleeting* mention. Pink cards joined the blue cards.[6]

As stated earlier, my observations have led me to conclude that the fame motive is insatiable. The following is from a conversation about two famous college professors.

> But it doesn't happen to everybody. [_____] wanted to be even more famous the day he died. He wanted to be just the most important person in the world. And there's [_____], also. He died bitter. He wanted to be the most famous. I mean, there are so many men—you can't satiate them.

This insatiability applies to even the most famous. "I want to be famous everywhere," said Luciano Pavarotti. Arthur C. Clarke, surely one of the most famous authors of the latter half of the twentieth century, described his need for continuous reassurance that praise and recognition earned in the past continues unabated in the present: "Clarke, . . . as almost everyone knows, moved some 40 years ago to live in Sri Lanka . . . By his own admission, he is a man with hunger for applause. 'Fame is the ultimate spur,' he says."[7] Clarke's most famous book, *2001,* has tens of millions of copies in print, but shortly before his death in 2008, he said he was writing the book (*3001*) that would make him famous.

How Far Does Fame Travel?

Big fame travels widely, especially now that it can be rapidly globalized through the mass media. In Picasso's words, one with such fame can "sit at the big table."

Small fame does not travel well, often not at all. The author of a just-published book was invited to appear on a local fifteen-minute television show. As it was about to begin, she learned she was in the middle slot, between a police sergeant who had made the most arrests in the prior month and the "Dog of the Week," selected from the local pound as its top candidate for adoption. Irwin Edman, famous some years ago as a professor of philosophy at Columbia University, described an experience on a lecture tour. He found himself in a Texas town as the middle "performer" in a local event. The manager told him, "The philosophers always come on after the acrobats." Nathaniel Hawthorne writes in his introduction to *The Scarlet Letter,*

> My fellow-officers, and the merchants and sea-captains with whom my official duties brought me into any manner of connection, viewed me in no other light, and probably knew me in no other character. None of them, I presume, had ever read a page of my writing, or would have cared a fig the more for me, if they had read them all; nor would it have mended the matter, in the least, had those same unprofitable pages been written with a pen like that of Burns or of Chaucer, each of whom was a Custom-House officer in his day, as well as I. It is a good lesson— though it may often be a hard one—for a man who has dreamed of literary fame, and of making for himself a rank among the world's dignitaries by such means, to step aside out of the narrow circle in which his claims are recognized, and to find how utterly devoid of significance, beyond that circle, is all that he achieves, and all he aims at. I know not that I especially needed the lesson, either in the way of warning or rebuke; but, at any rate, I learned it thoroughly.[8]

Even the fame of Nobel laureates may not go far. A woman being introduced at a party to a winner of the Nobel Prize asked him, "What is that?" Along the same lines, a *New Yorker* cartoon shows two women having tea as one addresses her husband, who is sitting near them with a pipe and reading a book: "It was just that one time that you won the Nobel Prize, wasn't it, dear?"[9]

Sometimes, people will be aware that a person is famous without knowing the reason. *Webster's Ninth New Collegiate Dictionary* lists about fifty-three hundred names of living and deceased individuals of varying degrees of fame from all parts of the world, as a reference for the spelling and pronunciation of their names.[10] Out of curiosity, I took a 25 percent sampling of the list to see how many names I recognized. It turned out that in my sample of 1,325, only 265 names were known to me. (By extrapolation, I would have recognized 1,060 among the 5,300). For most of the names I recognized, I knew what deeds had made them famous. For others, I knew the areas of their achievement, but not specifically what they had done. There were a few names I had certainly heard of, so they must have been famous, but I had no idea why. This highly personal and unscientific study made me think that if we recognize a name at all, we're likely to know why that person is famous or at least the field of his or her achievement; but sometimes only the name will ring a bell, probably faintly and with nothing to follow.

To become famous at all is to triumph over great odds. To become widely famous and for a protracted period of time is truly extraordinary. Yet the public's ignorance, indifference, misinformation, or confusion about all but the most celebrated figures of a generation can be profound. It is said that when world-famous violinist Jascha Heifetz encountered a blizzard on one evening during a concert tour of the United States, only a handful of people showed up to hear him play. The virtuoso's contract released him from performing before so small an audience, and the concert was canceled. A man called out from the audience, "Oh, come on Jascha, at least sing one song. We drove forty miles to hear you." When you become famous in one place and then, by choice or necessity, travel to another, your fame may be left behind. In an interview, a U.S. Army officer who had served in Europe described his experience at the end of his tour of duty.

> I had enough combat in that I would have come home pretty fast or gone to school over there, but I signed them away and came back to, and joined a green outfit. And I walked out from under my legend, or my reputation, or whatever it was—my fame—which was a guy who in

combat, you know, had a legend going, so that when I went to the mess line, the food would be there and people volunteered to be my driver, because I was the one guy in the outfit who was generally always in the front lines or else in the aero-p's. I was a recon guy.

People were talking about you?

They had a legend, some of which they had built up themselves. And I had been commissioned on the battlefields, so I was an enlisted man in their perception. And enough of the people who had known me as a sergeant were still around. Then I walked into this artillery unit of strangers and people who hadn't been in combat, and they didn't know me, and suddenly I don't have anything. I go out to take reveille the first morning of my battery—my assigned battery Baker—and did my usual thing when the first sergeant reported all present and accounted for. So I gave him a, you know—I flipped off a quick salute and said, "It's all yours, Sarge," and walked away very unmilitarily but very "cool," to use modern terminology, which everybody would have kind of laughed about in my old outfit because of the legend that went with me as pretty nonchalant and pretty entertaining. I had 116 missions over the lines or behind them, but that didn't mean a thing to this crowd. You know, who is this little teenager—teenage officer who doesn't even have a beard? I smoked a pipe so as to cover up my age. And that afternoon in softball, I've never been a good hitter and I struck out, so that all the chances I had to be a presence in this new outfit faded away. And the next day, I'm in Baker pen in service battery—you know, the truck that hauls the ammunition and food. The idea of me being in service battery was such a shock that I couldn't understand it. And it took about a month to get service battery so that they were the best drill team, you know, in the battalion, and begin to work my way back to being me. Partly because a sergeant from my old outfit showed up and said, "Do you know who that is?" And that helped a lot.

Fame seekers with minor fame will always want to make themselves known to a larger audience. Unlike Luciano Pavarotti or Arthur Clarke, who kept enlarging their fame through a long string of successes, they may attempt to do so without any new and recent achievement, simply by proclaiming to a new audience what they've already done. When trying to increase the size and number of groups and places where one is recognized, one will often overvalue one's record or misread how it will be received by the larger audience, with the result that he or she will be ignored or rejected. If the person ends up relatively less famous in the new setting than before—a small fish in a bigger pond—the entire attempt may backfire, leaving him or her more needful of acceptance and approval than before the attempt was made.

A different case, I think, is when someone wants attention for being famous from an in-group, where everyone knows the individual. This often occurs among men in their families. The paterfamilias wants to be valued for being famous beyond the family group. But this does not always work. Hence, a popular kitchen sign reads, "He may be a big chief downtown, but he's just another Indian around here." In one instance, when an internationally known psychologist was trying to squeeze more recognition from his rather difficult wife, she went to a party alone and, on returning, said to him triumphantly, "And do you know what? There was nobody there who had ever heard of you." Shortly afterward, they were divorced.

Summary

- The audiences we create or select when we seek to be famous may at first, in childhood and youth, be vague and unspecific.
- In time, the fame motive is directed toward identified special groups of people. These may be small or large, single or numerous.
- Even at the pinnacle of fame, people still want a larger audience, a bigger gallery of witnesses.
- People of minor fame who want to reach to a new and larger audience may attempt to do so without any new achievement, simply presenting their existing achievement(s) as credentials. They rarely succeed.

9 ☆ Making Fame Last

Early and Late Fame

There are no timetables for the arrival of fame, which can occur at almost any age. This fact is fundamental to understanding the fame motive, for it means that those who are driven by it can go through life dreaming of becoming famous. I asked a friend, "Well, have you ever toyed with the idea, yourself, of wanting to be famous?" He responded, "I think I've said to you—we used to joke about it when I was, you know, twenty-eight years old. I said, 'Well, I'm trying to get on *Time,* the cover of *Time* magazine, by the time I'm thirty'; then I said thirty-five, then I said forty. I don't know if I was joking or what, but when you're young and ambitious, and you're doing things which, you know, in your perception (I mean, you're succeeding, you're having some success in some things), there are always fantasies of—I don't know, at least there was for me—there were fantasies of recognition."

Some careers are orderly, with clear steps of progression. A pure case is that of a career soldier, which specifies an orderly sequence of advancement through a twenty-year period. For certain occupations, there are studies of career trajectories and the average age of highest achievement, with the familiar concepts of "early climax" and "late bloomer" referring to the times before and after such peaks. Other timetables are based on the physical demands of one's work.

More than fifty years of research by social scientists on the age of "greatest creativity" has been analyzed by Simonton.[1] The works of scientists or artists judged by their peers as most original and valuable were matched with the age at which they were produced. The results show that while creative output tends to rise fairly rapidly through the years to a definite peak, it declines afterward, until productivity is about half of what it was at the top.

The age of peak performance varies widely. At one extreme, some fields are characterized by relatively early peaks, usually around the early thirties or even late twenties, with somewhat steep descents thereafter to an output rate of perhaps less than a quarter of the maximum. This age pattern holds for such fields as lyric poetry, pure mathematics, and theoretical physics. At the other extreme, the trends are more leisurely, rising to a peak in the late forties or even the fifties chronologically, with little, if any, drop-off thereafter. This more elongated curve holds for such fields as medicine, philosophy, the writing of history, and general scholarship.

Of course, many careers are essentially episodic. In these, the relationship between age and achievement is not predictable. At the beginning of a year on Wall Street, in corporate finance, you don't know what deals you will do, with and for whom, or what resources you'll need. In politics, there can be a steady rise up the party hierarchy, or circumstances can produce elevation to prominence at an early age, late in life, or never at all. Success in show business and in literary careers tends to come early, with a falling-off to follow, unless the performer or author is adept at anticipating or responding to changes in public taste, in which case it can last for decades.[2]

Some people are famous early in their lives. Actress Carrie Fisher had extraordinary success in her early years in films. She said, "You live faster. You get there sooner . . . I was world-weary at 20. I had unlimited access, money, fame and acceptance."[3] And authors: J. London writes, "Jack London (1876–1916) was born in poverty in San Francisco . . . By the age of twenty-nine, with the publication of *The Call of the Wild, The Sea Wolf,* and *White Fang,* he was the highest-paid and most widely read writer in America . . . Unable to match the success of his early works, however, and plagued by alcoholism and rheumatism, he died of an overdose of morphine at the age of forty."[4] Fifty years later, Jack Kerouac's publication of *On The Road* (1957) "hurtled him into instant international fame—household-word fame that he couldn't handle and gradually lost, but not before it cost him his dearest friendships, the fulfillment of his artistic promise, and his personal freedom in the twelve years remaining until his alcoholic death, in 1969."[5] The late Italian novelist Alberto Moravia was interviewed by several people about his first book, *Gli Indifferenti.*

Interviewers: Will you tell us something about it?

Moravia: What do you want to know? I started it in October 1925. I wrote a good deal of it in bed. . . . It was published in '29.

Interviewers: Was there much opposition to it? From the critics, that is? Or, even, from the reading public? . . .

Moravia: Oh. . . . No, there was no opposition to it at all. It was a great success. In fact, it was one of the greatest successes in all modern Italian literature. The greatest, actually; and I can say this with all modesty. There had never been anything like it. Certainly no book in the last fifty years has been greeted with such unanimous enthusiasm and excitement.

Interviewers: And you were quite young at the time.

Moravia: Twenty-one. There were articles in the papers, some of them running to five full columns. It was without precedent, the book's success. (*Pausing*) I may add that nothing approaching it has happened to me since—or, for that matter, to anyone else.[6]

People seeking fame want it early. David Giles describes Morrissey, a pop singer in England who became famous at about age twenty-four: "Morrissey . . . deserves a place in history simply for trying so hard to be famous, and achieving his aim in the end . . . By the age of 18, he was becoming increasingly hungry for fame, and a scribbled note from this period reads: 'I'm sick of being the undiscovered genius, I want fame NOW, not when I'm dead.'"[7] If fame doesn't come early in life, expectation must be changed, and hope must be transferred to later years. In *Ambition*, I wrote,

As we travel farther through the lifespan, and our dreams have not yet come true, we can take heart from the experiences of others. We think of the sweetness of success that might yet come—winning after you thought you had lost. We note the many authors, photographers, performers, actors, composers, whose work was not rewarded until long after it first became public. Dancers point to the late Margot Fonteyn; writers, to Daniel Defoe who wrote *Robinson Crusoe* at age fifty-nine. Abel Gance's 1927 film *Napoleon*, unnoticed when it first appeared, was resurrected for a 1981 film festival revival and acclaimed a masterpiece. Gance, then ninety-three years old, had a year of triumph before he died. A novelist, Helen Hooven Santmyer, for 50 years had been writing a 1300-page novel about life in a small town in Ohio. At age 88 her book *"And Ladies of the Club"* became a best seller and was chosen as a main selection of the Book-of-the-Month Club.[8]

As an author and politician, Winston Churchill became famous before he was thirty, and he was Great Britain's wartime First Lord of the Admiralty before he was forty. Yet here is what a contemporary wrote about him then.

> As an administrator Winston Churchill has been cautious to excess and followed his chief war adviser, Admiral Lord Fisher, very closely . . . [N]o great or original stroke of genius need be expected from him in any place . . . He reads only to prepare his speeches and has no other artistic tastes. But, on the other hand, he is easy of approach and his heart is in his work; he listens to everyone, even though he cannot grasp all that is said to him; in fine, he is an excellent subaltern: capable, industrious, and supremely courageous, but not a pathfinder or great leader of men.[9]

For nearly twenty-five years after that time, Churchill's reputation and career experienced a steady decline, until he was close to being counted out as a political force. Not until World War II, when he was sixty-five and his country was facing defeat, did Churchill's extraordinary powers of leadership lift him to the heroic level of fame, where millions still place him.

As one ages, the belief that one can become famous in one's lifetime weakens in the face of accumulating evidence that it's not going to happen. For some, the emphasis then shifts to becoming famous after death. Says one person, "I have gone in for posthumous discovery." Does posthumous discovery occur? Schopenhauer writes,

> Any circumstances which may have prejudiced them in their origin, fall away with the lapse of time. Nay, it is often only after the lapse of time that the persons really competent to judge them appear—exceptional critics sitting in judgment on exceptional works, and giving their weighty verdicts in succession. These collectively form a perfectly just appreciation: and though there are cases where it has taken some hundreds of years to form it, no further lapse of time is able to reverse the verdict;—so secure and inevitable is the fame of a great work.[10]

Echoing this, a friend in our discussion refers to the genetic discoveries of the monk Gregor Mendel: "Fame can happen long after the subject has died. Perhaps the extreme and rare case is of the person (or object of fame) who is entirely obscure during his own lifetime but long afterward becomes famous—fame is conferred retroactively because value is not recognized earlier." To become famous after death can be a powerful ideal. In *Ambition,* I wrote about Robert Wilson's research on poets: how they can continue to write poetry without recognition or reward from friends or peers and in the face of negative criticism of their work—sustained by the conviction that generations still to be born will brush aside this rejection and hail them as great poets.[11]

We might think that few sociologists expect to become famous after death. But a study by Frank R. Westie of his fellow American sociologists found that about 40 percent expect to go down in history as among the top ten in their field of specialization. At the time of his research, there were more than ten thousand sociologists in the United States and about twenty such fields—meaning that only about two hundred top ten rankings were available to the four thousand who expected to be included in them. Comparing those who had been in the profession for more than twenty years and might be more realistic about their chances of becoming famous with those who had just entered it, Westie found no difference. Instead of lowering their aspirations for fame, the older sociologists simply extended their timetables for achieving it. With the criteria for evaluating achievement as a sociologist being uncertain, even fuzzy, it was easy for them to believe that their work would earn them top-ten recognition, if not in their lifetimes, then surely from a discerning posterity.[12]

Braudy, in his history of fame, writes about one of the Enlightenment's notorious fame seekers, Jean-Jacques Rousseau.

> Disgusted with theater, virtually unable to speak in front of any public audience, Rousseau tells us he wants to be free of public opinion, but only to seek another public, in posterity, reachable only through the book: "Even today, when I can see the most baleful and terrifying plot that has ever been hatched against a man's memory advancing unchecked towards its execution, I shall die a great deal more peacefully, in the certainty that I am leaving behind in my writings a witness in my favour that will sooner or later triumph over the machinations of men."[13]

On his powerful desire for fame as a scientist, Sigmund Freud wrote,

> I sacrificed unhesitatingly my budding popularity as a physician and a growing practice in nervous diseases because I searched directly for the sexual origin of their neuroses . . . but the silence which followed my lectures, the void that formed about my person, and the insinuations directed at me, made me realize gradually that statements concerning the role of sexuality in the etiology of the neuroses cannot hope to be treated like other communications . . . but as my conviction of the general accuracy of my observations and conclusions grew and grew, and as my faith in my own judgment and moral courage were by no means small . . . I was imbued with the conviction that it fell to my lot to discover particularly important connections, and was prepared to accept the fate which sometimes accompanies such discoveries. This fate I pictured to myself as follows: . . . science would take no notice of me during my lifetime. Some decades later, someone would surely stumble upon the same, now untimely things, compel their recognition and thus, bring me to honor as a forerunner, whose misfortune was inevitable. Meanwhile, I arrayed myself as comfortably as possible like Robinson Crusoe on my lonely island. When I look back to those lonely years . . . it seems to me like a beautiful and heroic era.[14]

Decay of Fame while Alive

At whatever age individuals may achieve fame, they almost always see it diminish before they die. Meanwhile, the fame motive will remain as strong as ever. Some may acknowledge their loss of fame to others with a debonair "Easy come, easy go." But beneath the surface, the loss will have reopened the wounds of long-ago rejection in childhood or adolescence. It hurts! These lines from the novel *Replay* describe how much.

> " 'Well, all right!' Becher said from the stage, wiping the mouthpiece of his clarinet. "Now, this next one is really what the blues is most about. You see, there's some blues for folks ain't never had a thing, and that's a sad blues . . . but the saddest kind of blues is for them that's had everything they ever wanted and has lost it, and knows it won't come back no more. Ain't no sufferin' in this world worse than that; and that's the blues we call 'I Had It But It's All Gone Now.' "[15]

Of someone once famous, we may hear, "He died a forgotten man," "His accomplishments have been swept down a hole of obscurity," or "She died unknown and penniless, her earlier fame forgotten." We say, "You're hot and then you're not," and we ask, "Where are they now?" We often witness descents from the heights of fame with the mixture of pity and grim satisfaction so well expressed in the German word *schadenfreude*. *People* magazine even had a section titled "Ever Wonder What Happened to So-and-So?"

We can lose assets that we haven't won but were born with and take for granted: good looks, a sharp mind, a strong constitution. We can lose assets that we partly won and that partly came our way as we grew older: promotions, pensions, inheritances. But most often, we lose what we actually have won: a job, a home, money, friends, love, power, prestige, fame.

How much can we really keep of what we've won? Wealth can be eroded or lost, houses deteriorate, beauty fades, and bodies weaken. To stave off entropy, maintenance never ends. So it is with fame. It can be sad times as one slides downhill toward being forgotten, whether one's fame lasted a day, a week, a season, or a decade. During the telecast of the Hollywood Oscars ceremony on February 29, 2004, artist Andy Warhol (1928–87), the author of the saying, known everywhere, "In the future everyone will be world-famous for fifteen minutes," was mentioned in an advertisement for Allstate Insurance, which began, "Someone once said, 'Everyone will be famous for fifteen minutes.'" The phrase lives on—it's now public property—but Andy Warhol, within fifteen years of his demise, had been reduced to "someone."

Decay of fame varies by occupation. In the case of athletes, one can be famous as an ocean sailor as late in life as age sixty. But in most sports, fame often declines quite suddenly, as the athlete passes his prime or simply graduates from college. One of John Updike's poems, "The Ex-Basketball Player," describes the rise and fall of early fame, and one of Irwin Shaw's best-known stories, "The Eighty-Yard Run," centers on a college football star who is unable to live up to his exploits in the years that follow.[16]

For some athletes, however, the picture has brightened considerably, thanks to the enormous interest in professional sports stimulated and sustained by television. As a spinoff, it has enabled many retired athletes who were only moderately famous when in their prime to maintain a foothold on fame (and earn a good living, too) as sports commentators, hosts or guests of sports programs, speakers at banquets, endorsers of products, and authors of books (usually ghostwritten) about their sport and themselves. All this is in addition to more traditional pursuits of over-the-hill athletes, such as coaching, opening a restaurant, and occasionally politics (e.g., former Philadelphia Phillies pitcher Jim Bunning was elected as a U.S. senator from Kentucky in 1998, and former Buffalo Bills quarterback Jack Kemp served nine terms as a U.S. representative from New York and was a Republican candidate for vice president in 1996). Former star athletes capitalizing on their diminished fame are so ubiquitous in American life that it comes as something of a shock to realize that two of the most famous athletes ever—Olympic swimmer Mark Spitz and tennis star Pete Sampras—retired when still in their prime and have done little to attract public attention since. Both, it seems clear, lack the fame motive.

A unique few experience little or no decay of their fame: they are those whose achievements are first-time, precedent-shattering performances. Roger Bannister, who broke the four-minute mile mark, and Chuck Yeager, the first in flight to break the sound barrier, became instantly famous. Though faster miles have since been run and though astronauts go faster in the sky, they—like Galileo, Gutenberg, and George Washington—have secured a place in history for being the first.

One would assume that fame achieved early in life would be particularly vulnerable to decay. There is a conspicuous exception, however: if early fame is succeeded by early death. When asked by Bernard Weinraub, "Why do [Marilyn] Monroe's life and legend have such a grip on the American psyche?" Jeanine Basinger, a film scholar, replied, "For one thing, she's dead . . . Were she alive today she would not look so hot."[17]

The especially glamorous kind of fame that emanates from a brilliant career cut off by untimely death, far from being a modern phenomenon, extends from Alexander the Great through Mozart to Princess Diana. By a unique historical coincidence, in early nineteenth-century England, it was the common fate of three great poets: Lord Byron, Percy Bysshe Shelley, and John Keats. They were contemporaries, born within seven years of each other. All were extremely handsome, were beloved by women, and made their marks early. At age twenty-four, Byron became famous. It was about the same for Shelley, and fame came about even earlier for Keats. Their deaths were as romantic as their poems. At age thirty-six, Byron died of malaria while fighting in the Greek War of Independence. At thirty, Shelley was drowned while sailing off the Italian coast; his body was burned on a funeral pyre. After a long struggle with tuberculosis, Keats died in Rome at age twenty-six.

There can be no doubt that the fame motive was strong in Byron and Shelley. Both loudly embraced radical politics. Shelley proudly proclaimed his atheism and urged it on others. The scandalous private lives of both men were defiantly acted out in public, to the point where England became too hot for them. Keats was different. Unlike the other two, he was of humble stock. His father operated a livery stable, and he had only one known romantic attachment. One might assume that he lacked the fame motive—until one encounters his tombstone. The poet designed it himself, specifying that it carry no name, no dates, only the words "Here lies one whose name was writ in water." In my view, this might be called a passive-aggressive reaching for fame. Much more than a plain "John Keats, 1795–1821," the mystery conveyed in those evocative and strangely self-deprecating words seem designed to make the passerby pause and wonder, "Whose grave is this? It must have been someone remarkable. How old was he? What did he do?" It is an indirect way of saying, "Look at Me!" Like the celebrity who is asked for an autograph and casually inquires, "How did you recognize me?" (knowing that it will elicit a torrent of praise), Keats knew what he was doing.

Considering these high achievers of fame invites a speculation: suppose one of the three had lived on? In Byron's case, English author and caricaturist Max Beerbohm has suggested an answer. His drawing shows an easy chair in a London club occupied by an irascible-looking elderly gentleman in mid-Victorian dress with a sizable belly and dyed hair—the very picture of self-indulgent privilege. The three-word caption slyly reads, "But for Missolonghi," referring to the place in Greece where Byron died. In the artist's view, after winding up a career that inspired the adjective *Byronic,* the 6th Baron Byron would have reverted to aristocratic type, taken his seat in the House of Lords, and become a firm reactionary. His fame might then be no greater than his more conventional contemporaries Samuel Taylor Coleridge and William Wordsworth—also great poets but whose powers declined as they lived on into their sixties and eighties, and who died without incident.

Both the reasons for loss of fame and its consequences include some variations worth examining. First, the achievement that brought fame may be surpassed by someone else. The audience then shifts its attention to the new champion and loses interest in the old one.

Second, the audience that confers fame may be age-related, made up, for example, of high school students or first-time parents or cancer survivors. As the audience grows older, it turns to new interests or concerns and falls away or disappears. Its replacement, should one emerge, is more likely to bestow fame on someone new than to adopt the choice of its predecessors.

Third, fame may be attached to a certain office or position, rather than to the one holding it. When one becomes the former CEO, Little League coach, or postmaster, mainly through retirement, obscurity quickly follows. In the 1960s and '70s, when he was head of the Metropolitan Museum of Art, Thomas Hoving was one of New York's liveliest and most media-savvy public figures. After leaving the post, he did little that was newsworthy and soon was mentioned only rarely. Former New York mayor Edward I. Koch, by contrast, left office rather unwillingly and successfully kept his name before the public over the succeeding twenty years, through talk radio, cultivation of the media, and authorship of books and quotable advice and criticisms. To anyone who might listen, he is ready to say, "Look at Me!"

Fourth, the achievement that brought fame may turn out badly—being a mistake or even a calculated deceit—and fame is thus stripped away and replaced by infamy. The local politicians, civil servants, architects, and contractors who were hailed as construction began on Boston's "Big Dig" expressway were reviled during the years of delay, inconvenience, and cost overruns that followed. John Eleuthère du Pont had promised five million dollars to Villanova University, and a sports arena had been built in his name. Subsequently, he was convicted of murder, and the university removed his name from the building. While amassing a great fortune, Alberto Vilar contributed many millions of dollars to the Metropolitan Opera, including several complete productions paid for by him and credited to his name. Then the tide turned, and he was arrested for money laundering and fraud. The Met dropped him from its list of supporters, and an article described his name as "slowly being erased from the annals of philanthropy."

Fifth, fame may be bestowed in advance in completion of an extraordinary achievement that doesn't materialize. In an interview, a newly published author explained, "You're up there and getting a certain amount of attention that you haven't had before, but that can be negative, because if your books then are not really selling all that well, there you are with everybody knowing the air's running out of the balloon. You suddenly have called attention to yourself. But you know you can't keep glossing it the way you hoped you would. You know, it isn't going up, up, up. I mean, you've achieved something. You've got all this attention—'Okay, here I am, everybody!' They're all looking at me, right? But, oops, it isn't quite going the way I wanted it to. They're all looking at me, and they all know now that I'm not going to be a famous author like—I'm not Jane Austen after all."

Sixth, after one or two exceptional achievements, a famous individual may be unable to follow through with others of equal merit or appeal. As evidence of nonachievement piles up, the audience turns away from someone it increasingly sees as a has-been. Samuel Johnson observed,

> A successful author is equally in danger of the diminution of his fame, whether he continues or ceases to write. The regard of the public is not to be kept but by tribute, and the remembrance of past service will quickly languish unless successive performances frequently revive it. Yet in every new attempt there is new hazard, and there are few who do not, at some unlucky time, injure their own characters by attempting to enlarge them.[18]

Much more desirable, of course, would be a gradual increase in the quality of one's work over a lifetime, so that one maintains or even increases the fame earned at the beginning.

The truth seems to be that, more often than not, the achievement that brings recognition and fame is probably the person's best work, likely to occur early, and not likely to be representative of the rest of the person's output. This might be called the Orel Hershiser Theory, referring to Hershiser's record-setting pitching performance for the Los Angeles Dodgers in the 1988 league playoffs and World Series, which he never managed to repeat. As for the golfer David Duval, he was once ranked number one in the world, but injuries over a period of years turned him into an also-ran. "Early last year a 12-year old girl at the Nissan Open tournament asked, 'Are you somebody?' 'I used to be,' he said." Scholar Harriet Zuckerman, a sociologist, in her study of Nobel laureates, says, "Just as baseball players rarely play well enough to be named most valuable player several seasons in a row and authors rarely write novel after novel of the highest distinction, so it is with laureates. Few of them continue to do research of Nobel caliber after the prize."[19]

Finally, fame can be lost when the achievement that produced it becomes detached from the achiever's name and then the name loses recognition. In science, it is customary to cite findings and publications by other scientists that one has made use of in one's own investigations. Over time, however, a finding that was cited when it was fresh and unusual will become absorbed into the science, and the citation will no longer appear. For example, in social research, the concept of "internal validity" is generally accepted as a standard for interpreting the results of a scientific study. For some time after being introduced and referred to, the term was put in quotation marks with a footnote citing the name of its creator. The next stage was for the term to appear without quotation marks but still with the footnote. The final phase came when it appeared without either, signaling that internal validity has become fully incorporated into our scientific culture.

Trying to Stay Famous

When confronted by the decay of their fame, the famous will usually battle to stay famous. The place in society where it's most fully understood that fame may be temporary is show business. Actress Greta Garbo sought to maintain her fame by retiring from the screen when her career, following the success of *Ninotchka,* was close to its height. There was more behind her retirement, however, than the failure of her next and last movie, *Two-Faced Woman.* An equal and probably more important factor was that Garbo's films had always been more popular in Europe than in the United States. In 1941, when she made her decision to retire, the European market, engulfed in World War II, had almost ceased to exist. This posed a threat to her future, starting with her status as a high-paid star. Rather than try to reshape her career into something different and probably less than it had been, Garbo preferred to walk away from it. After the war, she turned down starring roles in at least two major movies, living quietly in New York for the rest of her life. In her article "And Now, the 16th Minute of Fame; In the New Rules of Celebrity, Has-Beens Qualify," Caryn James describes the degradation of efforts to maintain fame. She writes, "Without seeing even one punch from tonight's 'Celebrity Boxing' show [between women] . . . it's enough to . . . know that . . . [these are] . . . quasi celebrities who have used up their 15 minutes and are playing in overtime."[20]

One way to try to stay famous is to succeed at something new. Maureen Orth, in her study *The Importance of Being Famous,* states: "Then there is the Queen Mother of all Reinvention . . . It is not only hard to get famous; it is even harder to stay cutting-edge. The pursuit and nurturance of fame is a job that can occupy the seeker 24 hours a day, seven days a week . . . Fame takes endless maintenance, fine tuning, damage control. It is a never-ending task, and Madonna has tackled it with a steely determination and zeal."[21] Another way is to do more intensely what brought fame in the first place. In a review of Andrew Sheehan's *Chasing the Hawk, Looking for My Father, Finding Myself*, Fred Waitzkin writes that his father, during the 1970s, wrote several best-selling books on running: "He became famous as a philosopher of the recreational running movement . . . he appeared on the *Tonight Show.*" Then thirty million people began running and the sport no longer was news. As his fame faded away, the elder Sheehan tried to maintain it by more writing, but without success. He is scarcely remembered today.[22]

A similar career is recorded by Kathy Watson in *The Crossing: The Glorious Tragedy of the First Man to Swim the English Channel.* Matthew Webb performed this feat at age twenty-seven in 1875, and it went unduplicated for thirty-six years. The author describes Webb as "probably the best known and popular man in the world" right after his deed, but before long he was forgotten. In an effort to restore his fame, he chose, against advice, to swim down the dangerous rapids in the river below Niagara Falls. He drowned in the attempt, a notable casualty of the fame motive, and was buried near the falls, in a place called Stranger's Rest.[23]

Fame after Death

Much-loved singer Peggy Lee quietly murmured, "If you leave a few songs, and a few people remember . . ." Others will do whatever they can to make sure that their fame outlasts them, ideally forever. But an enduring fame is always unlikely. Herbert Spencer (1820–1903), one of the most famous men of the nineteenth century, was more widely known and praised at his death than perhaps anyone who has lived. It is said that when he died, flags flew at half mast around the world. Yet who today remembers or has even heard Herbert Spencer's name. Philosopher George Santayana observed, many decades later,

> It must be exhilarating to stand on the hill-tops and point the way to future generations . . . Such prophets have their regard . . . But frankly, if in some respects Herbert Spencer's views have grown so obsolete, I think he deserved his fate. A philosopher should not be subject to the mood of the age in which he happens to be born. When a man swims to eminence and to joyous conviction on the crest of that wave, he must expect to be left high and dry at the ebb-tide.[24]

Those who leave behind works of art have an obvious advantage. The names of painters, sculptors, composers, and architects have a much longer shelf life than those of most political, religious, and commercial names of their era. Painter Will Barnett commented to me that he and his generation (now well over age ninety) were raised to believe that their art would survive them and that they could remain famous after death. He himself always used "the best materials," no matter how expensive, so that his work would last, and he felt further assured by knowing that a book of photographs of his most important paintings would be printed on acid-free paper that will last for generations.

In their study of artists, Gertrude and Kurt Lang say that "the durability of reputation is closely tied to the artists' leaving behind both a sizeable, accessible, and identifiable oeuvre and persons with a stake in their preservation and promotion." They note how artists strive to have their work placed in museums, even "specifically giving their work to a particular museum."[25] Having a larger body of work, the making of many reproductions of the artists' creations, the dispersal of these into many hands—all these factors raise the chances of remaining famous after death.

A solid first stop toward this goal is to be notable enough to have your death reported and your career summarized by a major newspaper. To be selected for an obituary in the *New York Times,* for example, is both an acknowledgment of one's fame and an assist in its survival (the selection process itself is discussed in the section "Fame Is Not Fair" in chapter 5). In a comprehensive study of obituaries prepared and published in the *New York Times,* the authors report the following:

1. Ninety-nine percent of the obituaries are of people in government and politics, the arts and media, and higher education; executives in business; and sports professionals.

2. When forty-two occupations are ranked by average length of obituary, "first, second, third, are members of Congress, singers, and judges," while "at the low end of the 42 occupations . . . are editors, lawyers, public relations, and advertising people."

3. Among 709,000 university professors, the chance of a *New York Times* obituary is 1.2 percent; among 93,000 authors, 4.9 percent; for 82,000 sports figures, 5.4 percent; for 74,000 lawyers and judges, 0.7 percent.[26]

More durable than a newspaper obituary is a listing in one of the international directories of famous people of the recent or distant past. From one or another of them, one can learn "who was who" at Waterloo, or during the reign of Louis XIV, or among Egypt's royal mummies. The best known directory is *Who Was Who in America,* a volume no longer limited to Americans but including world notables as well. According to the description on the publisher's Web site, "*Who Was Who in America* preserves the lifetime accomplishments of many world history-makers . . . Approximately every three years, sketches of *Who's Who* Biographees who have died since publication of the prior volume of *Who Was Who in America* are incorporated into a new compilation."[27]

Fame after death is helped by being included in such institutions as a Hall of Fame of some kind, which will last over time and preserve a member's achievements in the institution's records. Usually, it will be connected to one's locale or career, the place where one's achievements have been most visible. This may be a union, a charity, a company, an ethnic organization, or a university. Besides maintaining an enduring record, these places may stage periodic events where the member, alone or along with others, is remembered and celebrated.

For the mighty, nothing so parochial would be adequate. Historically, they have created their own memorials, in the form of monuments, temples, coins struck with their images, portraits, palaces, and statues erected to themselves. A friend commented on a book by Deyan Sudjic, *The Edifice Complex,* that part of the impulse to initiate and leave behind enduring monuments of architecture stems from the insecurity of people with towering egos (dictators, bishops, etc.), who are driven by the fame motive and haunted by the fear that they will be forgotten when they die. When Hitler arrived in Paris to lay claim to it in 1940, he insisted on being accompanied by Albert Speer, Herman Giesler, and Arno Breker. All three were architects, and Hitler's entire visit was devoted to discussions about demolishing the great buildings and monuments of Paris and replacing them with his own.

In New York City, Frederick P. Rose was a major builder of residential and office buildings. Rather than create new structures to memorialize himself and his wife, Sandra, he chose to improve or revitalize existing ones, building a new planetarium for the American Museum of Natural History and restoring the majestic Main Reading Room of the New York Public Library, among other projects. Britney Spears has a museum in her hometown; Dan Quayle in Indiana; Lawrence Welk in California; and Andy Griffith in North Carolina.

American hospitals have memorial plaques on rooms, equipment, even urinals, to honor people who gave money to the institution. This democratic custom makes preservation of one's name beyond one's death possible for thousands, not just the very rich who can afford to have a whole building or a stadium named for them. In an article entitled *Wanted: Contributors in Search of Immortality,* Kathleen Teltsch writes, "Universities and colleges will carve the name of a generous benefactor in limestone on an imposing building. Too costly? The donor can opt for a piece of the building."[28] The presumption is that one's fame will survive after death as long as the monument does. Still, poet Henry Austin Dobson raises a doubt in his rhyme "To an Unknown Bust in the British Museum."

> Far better, in some nook unknown,
>   To sleep for once—and soundly—
> Than still survive an wistful stone,
>   Forgotten more profoundly.[29]

Potentates not only leave huge burial memorials—the pyramids in Egypt and the tombs of Chinese emperors; they also leave their bodies. Clive James writes, "We have Alexander the Great, whose body was embalmed and kept on show at Alexandria; similarly with Lenin in Moscow and Mao Tse Tung in [Beijing]."[30] The most extreme case is that of Jeremy Bentham, an English philosopher. He left a fortune to University College London, specifying in his will that his body be displayed. A wax model was made of his head, and his skeleton was dressed in his clothes. His body was enclosed in a glass case, seated in a chair and wearing a hat, with his hands on his thighs. For many years, the case was conveyed to meetings of the college's trustees. It remains on display in the cloisters of the UCL Main Building.[31]

In contrast to the endeavors of persons intent on immortal fame are the simple efforts of those indifferent to fame who only want to have their memories recorded for their families and descendants. Mothers and fathers write long recollections of their early years before they met. These precious memoirs are seldom circulated beyond the extended family, perhaps fifty to seventy-five individuals. They are directed to the parents' descendants, to say to that unborn audience, "I was here. This is me."

Today, people can pay to have their biographies written and even published. There are also production firms, such as Hollywood Forever in California, that will create multimedia biographies of their clients. Some of these are made while the subject is still alive; others serve as video obituaries. The latter are generally ordered by the family, as a remembrance of one they loved, although living subjects tend to initiate such projects themselves.

Famous people whose fame has evaporated during their lifetimes will often hope for its resurrection after they die. More than most, authors have reason to think that this hope might actually be realized. As long as their books survive, they are subject to reevaluation by future generations. Andrew Delbanco writes about the case of Herman Melville. The publication of *Moby-Dick* in the nineteenth century was received with poor reviews and poor sales. Today, *Moby-Dick* has been resurrected as a classic. "Within, and beyond, the academy," observes Delbanco, "the resurgence of Melville from obscurity in his time into almost cult status in our own has been astonishing."[32]

That fame can be a roller-coaster ride of extraordinary heights and depths is epitomized in the career of F. Scott Fitzgerald. It's ironic that the author of the line "There are no second acts in American lives" should himself now be seen as the leading man in not just two acts but three. Act 1 opened with the publication of *This Side of Paradise* in 1920. It made Fitzgerald immediately famous. A week later, he married Zelda Sayre, and they began their elegantly madcap young life together. In 1925, with *The Great Gatsby*, he reached the crest of both critical and popular acclaim.

Act 2 began slowly, as for nearly seven years thereafter, Fitzgerald produced only short stories and lost much of his standing as a novelist. He expected to restore his reputation with *Tender Is the Night* in 1932, which he considered his best work ever. Not only did it prove a failure, but it was accompanied and followed by Zelda's confinement for serious mental illness and Fitzgerald's struggles with alcoholism. His career went steadily downhill, as he turned to doing hackwork in Hollywood to support his wife and daughter. He died there at age forty-four in 1940, without completing another novel.

Act 3 opened ten years later, with the publication of two best sellers, *The Disenchanted* and *The Far Side of Paradise* (the former fiction, the latter not), based on the combination of talent, glamour, and self-destructiveness that made Fitzgerald's life so dramatic. After twenty years of depression and war, the public had developed a retrospective interest in the carefree era of the Jazz Age, of which Scott and Zelda were symbols. With this came a rediscovery of his work, especially *The Great Gatsby,* now widely considered the great American novel of the 1920s. It became and remains required reading in literature courses, where it is studied by thousands of college students every year who are surprised and delighted by its romantic story and evocative prose, especially since, unlike the novels of Fitzgerald's contemporaries Sinclair Lewis and Theodore Dreiser, *Gatsby* is satisfyingly short. Today, nearly seven decades after his death, Fitzgerald's name and reputation hold steady around an all-time high. More than three hundred thousand copies of his books are sold each year. Act 3 is having a very long run.

As Fitzgerald's example illustrates, in the long run, lasting fame is not so much achieved by individuals—many of whom may not have sought it or even wanted it—as bestowed by society. In a commercial society, it's not surprising that the famous dead have also become commercialized. In a TV spot for the restaurant chain Applebee's, which specializes in barbecues and other food from a hot grill, we hear Peggy Lee singing perhaps her most famous song, "Fever." In a column entitled "Grave Revisionism," we read,

> In the past couple of years, everyone from Einstein to Ghandi has been given new life selling products. No doubt many of the exhumed, having achieved fame through the old-fashioned method of doing rather than promoting, are rolling over in their graves. By the time Madison Avenue gets through with them, we may have a tough time recognizing them. "Hm, was Einstein the one who sold computers or French fries?"[33]

Summary

- There are no timetables for becoming famous. Fame is associated with extraordinary achievements that may occur at any age.
- People seeking fame want it early, rather than late, in life.
- At the end of a career or near death, one begins to believe in the possibility of posthumous fame.
- Fame fades away. Most people who become famous during their lives are less famous—even forgotten and obscure—when they die.
- Confronted by the decay of fame people may have achieved in their lives, they struggle to stay famous. Many of their efforts are degrada-

tions of the paths to fame, from seeking a level of honor to strange and deviant acts.

· Much effort by famous people during their lives is given to maintaining their fame after death, through creating works that will endure in obituaries and archival records and establishing monuments and charitable foundations.

10 ☆ Coming to the End

Final Reality

I have described how persons motivated by fame can, at any age, see that they're not going to be as famous as they want to be. Others who have become famous often see that they are losing their fame; they have it but can't keep it. In response, both groups may have resorted to new methods—tried new paths—to become or remain famous. They may alter their timetables, giving themselves more years to reach their goals. Aspirations for worldwide, lifetime, and posthumous fame may be reduced to recognition by smaller audiences for shorter periods. The sustaining delusion of creating a unique, great work may have been abandoned but not yet given up.

Then there comes a point in life—whatever the age, whatever the level of strength of the fame motive, however much fame may have been achieved—when they see the end. A woman in midlife said, "I've already been as famous as I'm ever going to be." A fortunate few will never come to this point but will continue to enjoy the life they dreamed of—perhaps becoming even more famous—and die before it disappears. The rest, having tried, without succeeding, everything that their values will permit, must at last acknowledge to themselves that no more fame is in store. I call this the *final reality*.[1]

Recognition of the final reality may be gradual. Usually, diverse little episodes that accumulate over time—even many years—gradually intrude into consciousness, until a revelation occurs. An analogy from human biology can throw light on this process. Cumulative small changes may occur in our bodies—in the composition of the blood, the strength of the heartbeat, or the liver's capacity to store various chemicals. These changes don't show up in our behavior, because body organs make unperceived compensations to deal with them. Biologists use the concept *organ envelope* to describe an organ's functioning limit, within which it can be stretched. But once the stretching exceeds the limit and the organ collapses in what is called the *terminal drop,* the liver stops working, or the heart stops beating, and suddenly the underlying pathology becomes evident.

Baumeister describes how cumulative events are abruptly given a shared meaning, how a person's many complaints and misgivings may remain separate from each other until the moment of *crystallization,* or recognition, of their combined meaning, which can have an enormous subjective impact. In interviews about these transforming experiences, 89 percent of respondents say, "An important truth was revealed to me." In three-quarters of the cases, it occurred suddenly. To four-fifths, it took them by surprise. For some, the experience occurred within a minute; for two-thirds, in less than twenty-four hours.[2]

A fundamental point about facing reality is that the information about one's fame may be imperfect. The truth and clarity of the evaluations we receive differ tremendously. Athletes say, "When you walk onto the field, you are running into reality." For almost a century, baseball statistics in this country have remained the best-kept set of records about career performance and possibly about anything at all. The achievements of ballplayers are appraised daily by measurements whose meanings are agreed on by all. In some other parts of life—entrance examinations for elite universities, making money, selecting the first seven astronauts—the information also is clear. Also for stand-up comedians, who have no place to hide if the audience doesn't laugh.

In the social sciences, there is the Social Sciences Citation Index (SSCI), an indexing and abstracting service for close to two thousand scholarly journals in all areas of the social sciences. Among other data, it reports where and how often an author or article has been cited in those publications. This is used as a measure of current recognition, and I would say it is a measure of fame, because the SSCI is worldwide. Scientists can punch a computer and see the number of citations of their work and their names, rising or falling during the course of a career. To see their SSCI-reported citations decline is to see their fame decline.

Advertising research includes many surveys of name recognition and sometimes face recognition. One of these surveys reports on which celebrities are product endorsers. They change each year: new names that have become better known replace those that are fading into obscurity. Also, there is a survey of what fees are paid to celebrities to be guests at parties and how these fees increase or decrease from year to year. Just as one's fee for a professional performance tends to decline over time, so will the fee he or she can expect for a product endorsement. One will inevitably reflect the other, as a gauge of a performer's dwindling fame.

In most pursuits, however, individuals with the fame motive who want to appraise the sources and extent of their fame and whether it's rising or falling—for most, a fairly constant concern—have only incomplete and likely erroneous data to work with. Their beliefs and perceptions will be clouded by hope or fear in recurring spasms. They can be more or less famous than they suppose. For most—probably the vast majority—there will be a strong tendency to overestimate how famous they are and their chances to become even more so. Regardless of how flimsy the evidence may be, it will be interpreted to support this mindset. Fame seeking is not for pessimists.

Self-deception can also be encouraged by a lack of negative evidence. We may overestimate our fame, thinking, "They're talking about me." It is understandable that those motivated by fame will overestimate how famous they are and their chances for more fame. The motive guides the interpretation of whatever flimsy evidence is available. It is likely that others will not tell you the truth about where you stand. In trying to find out whether we are losing, we come up against situations in which other people know but will not tell us. Sometimes, we lose but do not know it. There are parties we were never invited to, love affairs that might have been but never got started—none of which are known to us. There are "short lists" for jobs never gotten by us: we can be evaluated for an open position, can almost win but be turned down, and never know this has happened in these and other ways. One can over time be downgraded by the world without being aware that it is happening. Social philosopher Sisela Bok writes in her book on lying, "Honesty is only one important aspect of human life. Another is not injuring people, which sometimes requires discretion and silence."[3]

There are also social constraints against acknowledging someone's fame. People may take for granted the fact that someone is famous, assuming that comment is neither needed nor wanted. As the following in-

terview excerpt reveals it would be no more socially appropriate to con-
gratulate someone for being famous than for being rich.

> *I'm thinking about why people don't congratulate people if they're famous.*
> *There's no feedback.*
>
> It's not a quality to congratulate anybody on.
>
> *If there were good works, you'd say it.*
>
> Of course.
>
> *You'd say, "Congratulations," and, "I compliment you on this noble deed*
> *that you did."*
>
> Yes.
>
> *But you wouldn't do it for money?*
>
> No.
>
> *Or fame?*
>
> No, no.
>
> *Or power?*
>
> Well, you could say, "My, you're a powerful person!"

There is also competition for fame. In theory it should be easier to find
out whether we're winning or losing in that race, since others should be
happy to tell us at least the former. But whether our immediate goal is to
win a promotion, impress a potential spouse, or be elected to office, our
competitors will never let us know if we have—or have lost—an edge.
Similarly, we don't tell others if they're ahead, thereby increasing their motivation and weakening our position. Keeping the competition ignorant is
to our advantage. We say in a fight, "Don't let the other fighter see he's hurt
you," and in contract negotiations, "Never let them see you sweat." Nor
would we ask our competitors for feedback about ourselves. Such naïveté
would only deliver us into their hands. For a reliable (and safe) appraisal of
our position it's best to rely on a mentor or a coach, a neutral member of
the team, or an informed friend who stands outside the competition.[4]
Sometimes you learn something by chance, in conversations (e.g., "She
called you a living icon [or a living legend]"; "You're famous—and much
loved too"; "But you're a big name"; "That was some book"; "But you are

very famous and he is not") or from reports (e.g., "He introduced you as a 'world-famous psychologist'"; "Everyone is talking about you"; "I saw you on television—a rerun I think").

Without clear feedback, we can misjudge what we've been accomplishing. We may slow down or even give up on a particular effort and then learn from an unexpected source—another part of the country, a surprise job offer, a mention on network television—that the sought-after fame had in fact been achieved. Meanwhile, we had assumed failure and started to try something else. "If only I had known," we say.

Information about one's fame is usually informal, incomplete, and probably inaccurate. Evidence is usually soft enough for even those with the fame motive to challenge its validity. Psychological research and our own observations show that if the information is unwelcome, we will try to avoid, distort, ignore, excuse, or discredit the substance of it—or even deny it altogether and fight back.

Still another way to deal with bad news is to rise above it by saying to others—and perhaps even more to oneself—"It doesn't apply to me." In professional baseball, an example of an occupation with well-established paths of career development, a player may decide that he simply is not going to follow the norms but will stake out his own route to the major leagues. Professional hockey players usually make it to the big leagues (or don't) by twenty-three, and if they do, they can usually play until twenty-nine. But a small number will maintain that level of play for twelve years, not six, and some young hockey players will ignore the odds and vow to be like them.

I myself have tinkered with evidence, trying to make it different. I thought that an earlier book of mine would find a major commercial publisher, but it didn't and instead was published by Basic Books, which specialized in the social sciences. I thought, "Well, good! It will stay longer in print that way," which would give the book more time to accumulate recognition for its merit and fame for its author. Alas, that didn't happen. Basic Books, for tax reasons, shredded my book early. Some years later, I was somewhat consoled when the Authors Guild selected it for reprinting by iUniverse, and now I find myself thinking that with my old book once again available, it may find a whole new public when this current book is published. The two books may generate word-of-mouth sales for each other and for their author and . . . well, you get the idea.

The case of Egas Moniz is described in Elliot S. Valenstein's *Great and Desperate Cures.*[5] In 1935, Moniz was a well-regarded Portuguese neurologist with a successful career behind him. His goal, however, was more than that. He wanted his name to be immortal. Desperate for a means to achieve this end, he conceived the surgical procedure of lobotomy, an operation to destroy the parts of the brain that he thought were the cause of mental illness. He promoted this procedure without definitive evidence of its effectiveness, and his first published reports claimed a high degree of success. Within a year or two, the lobotomy procedure had spread to other countries, and in 1949, Moniz's dream came true: he was awarded the Nobel Prize in Medicine. By 1960, however, following a decade of criticism and research that revealed its damaging, rather than benign, effects on most patients, the lobotomy operation had become rare. For Moniz, fame has become infamy.

Eventually, most of us see that we're going to be disappointed no matter what we do. Time is running out. Though we've tried working harder and done our best to work smarter, it's clear that we'll never win or keep the fame we've longed for, and we can't lower our aspirations further without settling for nothing at all. I wrote in *Ambition,*

> Just before accepting what seems to be our destiny, just prior to the acceptance of the fact that what is happening is inevitable, there is a wild and irrational search for new ways to deal with the impossible situation: a desperation move, such as resigning abruptly from a career, plunging in the stock market, trying to set up a love affair, making radical health habit changes. This is the "last chance syndrome"; the nearly busted crap shooter, putting everything he's left on the line for one last pass; the gold miner looking for the big strike in dangerous country before he dies.[6]

The chosen path to fame, selected earlier in life, is abandoned; there is degradation of behavior into bizarre attention-seeking actions. Fantasies may develop.

There are many studies of fans (the term *fan* comes from the Latin *fanan,* meaning "a temple, a place to worship," and from *fanaticus,* meaning "belonging to a temple"). The fame motive may be involved in one class of fandom, in which fans, if only in imagination, can share in the fame of their idols. Millions of people identify with celebrities, vicariously sharing their successes and failures, whether alone or as members of fan clubs. Many people identify with the heroes in the hard-boiled detective fiction of Raymond Chandler, Dashiell Hammett, Ian Fleming, and John D. MacDonald. Some biographers identify so closely with their subjects—James Boswell and Samuel Johnson, Ernest Jones with Sigmund Freud—that the two come to seem extensions of each other. With some people unchecked fandom can edge into the bizarre and in full-blown and elaborated form can become—as with stalkers—an incapacitating mental illness. Since nobody around you need know about your fantasy, which itself may not be vulnerable to actual experience, one can easily drift into an imaginary life. In the end you may go mad (fame seekers include plenty of crazy people) and actually believe you *are* the famous person you admire.

Trying to Escape

As noted earlier, not everyone who is rejected and in need of acceptance and approval turns to fame as consolation and fulfillment. Devotion to God, reliance on imaginary friends and imagined future events, even a dog's affection may fill the empty space. Ironically, those with the fame motive, as they age and begin to see that their aspirations will never be realized, try to rid themselves of the motive and its attendant dreams and replace them with adult versions of the compensations that others found in childhood.

Love from God

Simply defined, to seek fame is to seek love from an audience. Hence, it may seem no great departure—indeed, more worthwhile and even ennobling—to seek God's love instead. Some nineteen out of twenty Americans say they believe in God. To say that you "believe in" something is an ambiguous claim, but surely the concept that "God is love" is a part of the belief.

William James, in his study *The Varieties of Religious Experience,* records one subject's testimony.

> At that instant of time when I gave all up to him to do with me as he pleased, and was willing that God should rule over me at his pleasure, redeeming love broke into my soul with repeated scriptures, with such power that my whole soul seemed to be melted down with love, the

burden of guilt and condemnation was gone, darkness was expelled, my heart humbled and filled with gratitude, and my whole soul, that was a few minutes ago groaning under mountains of death, and crying to an unknown God for help, was now filled with immortal love, soaring on the wings of faith . . . I then closed my eyes for a few minutes, and seemed to be refreshed with sleep; and when I awoke, the first inquiry was, Where is my God? And in an instant of time, my soul seemed awake in and with God, and surrounded by the arms of everlasting love.

Another subject reported,

The Holy Spirit descended upon me in a manner that seemed to go through me, body and soul. I could feel the impression, like a wave of electricity, going through and through me. Indeed, it seemed to come in waves and waves of liquid love; for I could not express it in any other way. It seemed like the very breath of God. I can recollect distinctly that it seemed to fan me, like immense wings. No words can express the wonderful love that was shed abroad in my heart. I wept aloud with joy and love; and I do not know but I should say I literally bellowed out the unutterable gushings of my heart. These waves came over me, and over me, and over me, one after the other."[7]

Braudy describes St. Augustine's turning to God: "He is unaware of his hunger for a love that is to be satisfied, the attention of God which alone can fulfill the longing of the soul for glory"; "Only through the love of God can man strip himself of the need for public praise and glory." Following the saint's model came the holy men, the monks, the nuns, and hermits—all content with God's attention and in want of little else. But as Braudy notes, God's attention has not always been an enduring alternative to the search for fame. He refers to the "satiric stories about the grotesque activities of bishops, particularly their self-importance [and] their fame seeking."[8] Fame was conferred on the religious person, a development that grew tremendously, so that religious life on earth was rewarded in the same way as public life.

For a disappointed seeker of fame, an intensification of belief in God's love—perhaps even better, a conversion to it—may not be only logical. It may be comforting and reassuring as well. Unlike the love of a mortal audience, the love of a God of love will never fail or be withdrawn.

Love from a Person

A friend asked, "To the extent that the fame motive rests on the absence of love in infancy [and childhood], would it not be possible for it to be replaced by the receipt of unconditional love in later years?" As I and countless others have learned, the love and admiration of grandchildren may become a huge source of satisfaction. In later life, acceptance and approval from a source of the original rejection may prove helpful. This may involve becoming close to a mother, father, or siblings who turned away from you in earlier times or being accepted at a high school reunion because of improvements in style and appearance and other characteristics that had caused classmates to ridicule you earlier. But I suspect that such instances of acceptance later in life do little more than temporarily anesthetize the fame motive; without driving a stake through its heart.

After reviewing an assortment of the great love stories of fact and fiction, I have yet to find one whose bond is giving and receiving attention and approval denied in childhood. What sounds happiest of all would be to experience true and lasting love from another person—although even that may not be enough. In the Academy Award film *All About Eve,* the aspiring actress says about her audience, "They want you. Waves of love come to you. One hundred new people every night." Opera singer Leontyne Price reportedly said, "Once you get on stage, everything is right. I feel the most beautiful, complete, fulfilled. I think that's why, in the case of non-compromising career women, parts of our personal lives don't work out. One person can't give you the feeling that thousands of people give you."

Therapy

In compensating for denial or loss of fame, the critical task is to heal the inner wound and conclude that the never-going-to-be-famous self is worthy and lovable after all. Perhaps some people can generate self-respect through pride in their own, even secret, achievements, rejecting the judgments of these who found them of little value. They may reconstruct the past to make it consistent with their present sense of self. My friend Ray Bordner once said to me: "Time is a flexible concept in the human mind and the present and the future determine the past."

Not only one's own past but those of spouses or children or fellow workers can be rewritten as well. Different motives can be attributed to them than were there before. The attitudes of individuals and groups significant in one's past can be juggled in the mind; actual events may be ignored and sometimes even imagined—all to dovetail with one's current level of achievement and future prospects. It should be added that individual recall and reporting on one's life history is often more a phenomenon to be studied than a source of valid data about what actually occurred; there are few limits to self-deception.

Would clinical treatment be helpful to someone with a repressed desire for fame? Although the success of clinical/psychiatric intervention is continually challenged, it is well established as helpful in curing depression and almost certainly would expose the unfulfilled need for attention that underlies the fame motive. But is it depression that four million Americans with the fame motive suffer from as the shadows lengthen over their hopes for fame? Would anything really be gained by forcing them to realize that what they see as hope is almost certainly delusion?

I have been asked, "What can we do to tame this motive? Can or should parents, schools, the clergy, the media, or even the government take action? What should such action involve?" Should there be support groups, similar to Weight Watchers or Alcoholics Anonymous. There are groups for dealing with gambling or sexual addiction. Are there discussion groups concerned with eliminating the desire for money or power or good works? Are there any for eliminating or at least controlling the desire for fame? I think not. The following excerpt from an interview is instructive.

Do you think it's possible in that way to get rid of this motive?

I do. I have certain convictions that the process of self-examination with skilled professional help can take people past their demons. I believe in it. You have to be motivated. You have to be willing to look at yourself honestly, willing to make a concerted effort to change your behavior. But it requires a huge amount of treatment.

I've studied reports on intervention and do not find anything that deals with specific learned motives being extinguished through clinical intervention. No protocols. No stories.

Well, there certainly is literature about addiction. Like Alcoholics Anonymous, I mean.

I view alcoholism and weight gain as expressions; it is what lies beneath that needs to be dealt with. You say, with skilled help, you can understand yourself and rid yourself of the fame motive?

Well, especially if it is rooted in what we're suggesting it is rooted in, some deep need for attention, I do believe the process of psychotherapy—when people actually go back and relive that and experience the emotions connected to that—I think that is a freeing process for many people. You know, it's a scary journey, because it requires you going back to reexperience some of your greatest moments of vulnerability, but I think going back to do that can take some of the burden of it off of them. I was basically saying that I think another way out of the burden of the fame motive beyond digging deeply within yourself is to try to understand early life influences that nurtured this unhealthy thing. I think also that there is insight that comes from recognizing that all fame is fundamentally fleeting anyway, even if it is deserved, legitimate fame.

The person who escapes, by one way or another, from the fame motive can look at the past left behind. It may become dim in memory, and when revisited, many of the early dreams may seem unfamiliar, as if they belong to a stranger. One may ask, "Who was this person who once dreamed of being famous?"

Protecting the Self

Once it becomes clear beyond doubt that the fame we have sought, often for many years, will never be realized—or perhaps, even worse, has been lost and will never return—the effect can be devastating. Having to accept, once and for all, that we simply don't have what it takes brings on feelings of worthlessness and even shame. As the fears from infancy and childhood of being unaccepted and unwanted are awakened from their slumber, the ancient pain returns: one is still a failure.

What happens to an individual with a powerful motive that can be neither fulfilled nor extinguished? I find no cases dealing with this question in the clinical or psychiatric literature. Those studies deal with feelings and sentiments, good or bad, desired and undesired, but not with profound motives like love for a specific person or drives for power and money or fame.

Some with the fame motive may become humble and accept themselves as failures. They also may acknowledge the talents and achievements of peers who have succeeded, even those they once viewed as their equals or less in abilities. There appears to be a fundamental downward revision of the self-image. "I used to want to be famous," they may say. Are such conversions genuine, or does the fame motive still smolder beneath the portrayal of humility? In a television documentary of a Trappist monastery, a monk stares at the camera. "I have no wife," he says. "I have no children. I have been here twenty years and I have had no proof that God exists." As his expression changes, he looks perplexed and adds, "I sure hope God appreciates what I'm doing for Him." Under the guise of humility, the monk is calling attention to his achievement and himself. He finishes with a nudge to God: "Look at me!"[9]

Even while failure is taking over, defenses are being erected. From my observations, I have identified five psychological processes—five "cognitive strategies"—that people whose fame motive goes unfulfilled employ to protect their self-respect:

1. Restructuring conflicts

2. Attributions for failure

3. New social comparisons

4. Sour grapes

5. Devaluation of others

Some of these strategies are familiar to clinical and psychiatric theory. Others are drawn from psychology and sociology. I have here labeled and described them solely with reference to the fame motive.

Restructuring Conflicts

We all have multiple interests in life—family happiness, friendship, money, health, good deeds, power, personal pleasures. From time to time, coexisting as they do, some will reinforce others, but conflicts also will arise, especially when the time and effort required by one interest cause a neglect of the others. This is especially the case when a major interest in one's life is to become famous.

Regularly and sometimes almost constantly through their lives, those with the fame motive will trim their other interests to make room for it. But what happens when the moment of ultimate truth arrives, when it's clear that all hope of fame is gone? Some people swallowing this bitter pill—the more fortunate—will reverse their objectives. Fame will be discarded, even scorned, and other interests will take its place—often with an accompanying sense of relief. Said a young Chinese boy, "When I learned that I would never be famous, my life became quite simple and easy." After an interview with a woman in her eighties, I received this poem, which she had written very early in life:

Not Yet the Laurel

Why try, with bleeding hands, to force these gates?
  They will not open yet to such as you,
Unheralded, unsung, your voice unknown
  You of the many cannot join these few
Who, laurel wreathed, triumphant, go their way,
  So powerless to hold their fleeting day.
  Quiet your pleading voice, it is too soon
To cry despairing to an unlistening moon.
  Wait for a little while, you yet may win,
  May not be always outside looking in.

The poem was accompanied by this note:

I wrote this in Hollywood after attending a movie premier there one night. It was either just before or after my 13th birthday.
   Well, from the time I wrote the poem I was very stage-struck. I loved the theater always, and wanted to be in it, wanted to be part of it, wanted to be famous, and then pursued it. In college I was in theater and also spent a summer and a half at a summer theater in Gloucester. I did experience what it was like and became disillusioned in the kind of the things that went with it, was disenchanted. I was successful. I realized I could go on and, you know, struggle along with Broadway in the way my friends did. But I thought it was too big a price to pay. The competition and the jealousy and the insecurity of that world was very clear as I took part in it.
   So I transferred my career goals to something which was more productive and more private and that was play writing, dealing with the theater world but in a different way. Writing the plays, and becoming involved with our children, and over the years, community activities . . . was all I could do.

By the early 1990s, I had written or edited a dozen books on human development through the life span and was having dreams of success for my new book, *Ambition.* When my agent informed me that the only offer he had for it was from Basic Books, I was deeply disappointed. My fantasies had included a larger publisher, able and willing to provide a generous advertising and promotion budget, leading to exceptional sales for a book of its kind, with glowing reviews and quite possibly awards and honors to follow. As all this faded, like Prospero's "insubstantial pageant" in *The Tempest,* I began to reflect that my enduring desire to be a famous writer had in many ways been a heavy burden. It had caused me to quit a good job when only in my forties, so that I later had to restart a broken career. It had required my wife to give up some of her own hopes in life. I heard myself saying, "You aren't going to be a famous writer, and you don't have to be. Lay that burden down and just be yourself." Gradually, as the long-standing conflicts between working on the book that would bring me fame were eliminated and other interests had room to blossom, I began to feel a freeing sense of happiness.

Attributions for Failure

When people who have failed in some enterprise are asked why, the reasons they name are either external (i.e., "It was beyond my control") or internal (i.e., "There is no one to blame but myself"). Probably the most familiar external attribution is to blame bad luck or bad fortune and claim that others were lucky. We might say, for example, "Why do successful people claim they did it all themselves though it's obvious they were born with a silver spoon in their mouth?" We believe we would have been famous except for luck and can even cite the times when and places where something that did or didn't happen prevented us from having our name in lights or on a valuable patent or kept us from being elected to office.

A common alternative is to blame others whom we see as dishonest competitors who cheated and lied about us and thus brought about our failure. Moreover, we can speculate that more of this went on than we will ever know about—that there were hidden, deliberate obstructions to our successes. We may blame others for our own inadequacies: our parents, our teachers, our ministers, our mentors, our mates, and any others who may have damaged us through various biological, psychological, and social means. One may thus argue, "I should have taken a different path. It was not my fault; I got bad advice."

When we blame ourselves for failure—and in American society, with its strong Protestant-ethic tradition, this is far from rare—we will often blunt the mea culpa by speculating that if we had been of a different sex or race or age or appearance (perhaps taller or thinner), things might have worked out differently. Erik Erikson has said that the final task of life is one of integration, when one must accept the fact that life could not have been otherwise. This retrospective acceptance of fate is also an attribution of causality to forces other than oneself—meaning, in the present context, that no matter how much or how long one may have strived to be famous, one can't be blamed, in the final analysis, if one has failed. It could not have been otherwise.

New Social Comparisons

Social comparison involves comparing yourself with others to evaluate your standing among them in respect to some personal achievement or characteristic. As a rule, people who are under stress will compare themselves with others who are worse off and avoid comparisons with those who are doing better. Jutta Heckhausen and I made a study of this "downward social comparison" by asking a large national sample of adults of different age levels about problems they expected for themselves and for most other people of the same age in twelve areas of life, such as health, marriage, job, and so on. The findings showed that in all areas, the respondents believed that other people's problems were more serious than their own. This self-protective tendency to believe that other people are worse off than you are has been confirmed in a number of related studies. People try to avoid comparisons unfavorable to themselves.[10]

It's not surprising, then, that fame seekers facing permanent disappointment will find comfort in comparing themselves to others who have failed even more, while avoiding any comparisons with the more successful. This may include reviewing what one actually accomplished (as done by former athletes with their yellowed newspapers), adding it up, and comparing the record with the lesser accomplishments of one's peers. In a more radical form of self-protection, some will act to change the social milieu where their failure was played out, by changing jobs, moving to a new neighborhood or a different state, getting a divorce—whatever it may take to escape the surroundings where one was a loser.

Sour Grapes

Aesop's classic fable about the fox and the grapes describes one way in which we try to deal with our unfulfilled aspirations. We let it be known that those who succeeded while we didn't are unhappy and that the price they paid was ruinous. A friend who wanted to be rich but wasn't liked to say, "Old Man Smith may have eighty million dollars but he's all alone in his big office with holes in his stomach, eating milk and crackers." We may hint that the success of those we envy came about through deceit or luck; we may remark that they're also having troubles with their children and so on. All this helps us feel better about our own failure.

That fame is a burden is a common belief. "Uneasy lies the head that wears a crown" is how Shakespeare put it, and Cowen notes that "the stoics, many Christian theologians, Petrarch, Dante, Milton" say much the same.[11] The sour-grapes process employs this bit of folk wisdom as a kind of emplacement from which to launch missiles aimed at the desirability of fame, a position from which to criticize lack of privacy and the need for fences and guard dogs; the necessity of bodyguards; constant requests for money from relatives, charities, and strangers; being hounded by reporters and paparazzi; and the ever-present possibilities of kidnapping and extortion. It can seem much better to avoid such perils by leading a life obscure and unobserved.

The truth is that we have no scientific study of the satisfactions versus the troubles of becoming famous. The sour-grapes assertion that fame doesn't bring happiness may be false. But we're willing to believe it if it makes us feel better.

Devaluation of Others

Envy is defined by the *Oxford English Dictionary* as "to feel displeasure and ill will at the superiority of (another person) in happiness, success, reputation, or the possession of anything desirable."[12] It makes us want others to fail.

Beyond the passive hope that those you envy for their fame might come to grief is the urge to retaliate against anyone who may have blocked your path to fame. There are many ways to get revenge, to even the score. An item in a personality test is "I often wish someone I knew were dead." This is more than degradation; this is destruction. To be thwarted from reaching a desired goal has been a cause of crime throughout the ages—most notably when a rejected lover kills his or her rival, mistress, or both. The fame motive has led to no such crimes that I know of, but with fame itself seen in our media-saturated world as ever more desirable and attainable, they may not be far off.

The Damaged Life

Is the fame motive good or bad for a person? That question can't be answered with facts, for no scientific studies exist of the relationship between *being* famous and *being* happy, much less of the correlation of the fame motive with subjective well-being. A critic asks, "Can I really document the fact that the fame *motive* has pathological elements, aside from sporadic anecdotes or writings about people who seem obsessed with becoming famous?" About those people "who chronically fail to be famous, on top of their preexisting misery that led to the fame motive in the first place," another critic asks, "Are they criminals, suicides, chronically ill, on welfare, on drugs? Are those with the fame motive included in the twenty million with mental illness and serious maladaptation?"

Without offering answers to such sweeping questions, I will assert that my own observations lead me to believe that the fame motive seriously damages the possibility of a good life. A psychologist shared these thoughts from a friend: "I agree that the desire for fame is likely a destructive force in human affairs. I also surmise that even among those who managed to achieve fame their final gratification from it was inherently empty. Probably in most cases the journey is accompanied by tragedies for others (neglected children, cast-aside spouses, using or being used by colleagues), on top of the realization that the base need for acceptance and approval was not met anyway. Worse yet, fame is inherently fleeting, a realization that must inflict horrific pain on those who have sacrificed all for it."

How does the fame motive hurt the person who has it? First, it is not a noble motive. It is viewed by society as selfish and contributing little of value. A person who wants to be famous may actually share this view, as experience shows how seriously the fame motive can injure and even overshadow other, worthier values, such as health and family. Equally important, the fame motive may be poisonous to the sense of self. Those individuals who manage to seek, find, and maintain fame at levels reasonably satisfactory to themselves can enjoy the ego gratification that accompanies success. But as we've seen, they're a small minority of the fame-motivated population, the great bulk of whom find themselves fated, like the mythological Tantalus, to hunger and thirst for fruit and water forever out of reach. Sooner or later, unwelcome questions intrude. Is this yearning for fame good or bad, selfish or unselfish, right or wrong? What is one to think of oneself when the answers are all negative yet the yearning retains its hold?

Second, the "cognitive strategy" of blaming others for one's failures applies to all unsatisfied motives. For most of us, being passed over for a promotion or defeated for reelection or dumped by a lover will produce wounds that, in time, lose their sting. But when the fame motive is frustrated, there is no moving on. One remains trapped in a dead end of resentment and doubt, blaming or degrading others, unable to abandon a hopeless goal.

Third, all selfish motives have the power to injure other people. If others stand in the way, they will be avoided, thrust aside, or even destroyed. Consider the following comments made by contemporaries in interviews.

> And I think this is where his need for attention spilled over into his life of womanizing, and so he needed constant attention not only from his scientific peers but from women around him, and I think that it had devastating consequences to his wife, to say nothing of his children.

> Attention was certainly a big deal in life, and the womanizing that went along with it. And so he is an interesting example of this style in the sense of no matter how much recognition, acclaim, fame you get, no matter how many women you have gone after who have responded to you, it's never enough. It's never enough. And for those kinds of individuals, I would say, you know, entering their twilight years and anticipating their own demise, it must be tormenting. Just tormenting.

Fourth, the "cognitive strategies" described earlier will go beyond one's internal psychological processes to be expressed in behavior toward others. It becomes second nature to withhold admiration or even acknowledgment of their successes. To belittle one's rivals, associates, friends, even family members verges on the automatic. Mean-spiritedness of this kind is the public manifestation of the envy and anger so often encapsulated in the fame motive, and it taints relations with other people.

Fifth, because the fame motive is considered by most people to be a negative characteristic, viewed with wariness and distaste, a person with this desire will hide it. The person is compelled to screen the true self and cannot say that this is a primary motive in life. This may lead to denial and repression of the desire, like a deviant sexual motivation. They are guarded and cannot reach out in openness, honesty, and intimacy. It hurts significant others who could be close, who want love and friendship but are denied it by the fame-seeking person.

Trying to be famous may spoil your life, but succeeding may also spoil it. Much has been written and said about "the price of fame," though no formal studies exist—just observations and speculations. Fame brings the obvious rewards of money and power, but there are negative consequences as well. I will mention three here.

First is the envy that fame generates. The more your life goes well, the more resentment you may incur. Anthropologists refer to *tall poppy syndrome*, where, in some cultures, if you stand out, you are cut down. A friend said of his parents, "I can remember both of them talking about people they thought were just too big and mighty and were going to get their comeuppance; there is a whole mentality that people who do so well are ultimately taken down—in part by their own bad motives, but also because they have fueled so much resentment in others."

Second, fame creates adversaries: people who oppose or dislike the kind of achievement that made you famous. Bloland observes that the greater a celebrity's fame, "the more intense will be his or her disfavor in the eyes of some," and "this disfavor becomes a constant part of his or her awareness."[13] A friend said in confirmation, "Any time you're visible, you're vulnerable to having people like you and not like you. Look at our presidential elections."

Third, in my view, the saddest and most damaging effect of becoming famous is to find, at the end, that fame is still not the answer to your need for acceptance and approval. Whether denied, hidden below the surface of consciousness, or expressed in conscious stratagems of self-protection, the fame motive will shake off discouragement and continue to live. Consider an old man floating dangerously far out from shore in the ocean because he wants the strangers on the beach to ask each other who he is. Or consider the seven year old at the resort hotel who calls out "Look at me!" when about to dive into the pool. We may smile at their actions, but what they really deserve is our pity. Most of us, if we fall short of certain life goals, will settle for others more within our reach. But those with the fame motive have a goal that, in many cases, they can't even define and, except for a few, will never reach. Worst, this desire resists all attempts to treat it.

Summary

- There is a point in life—at whatever age and however much, if any, fame may have been achieved—when the end is in sight. One sees that no more fame is in store and that whatever fame one may possess is dying. This is the "final reality."

- Information about one's fame is informal, incomplete, and probably inaccurate. People with a fame motive will challenge the validity of unwelcome information as long as they can.

- Those trying to escape from the fame motive may try to find another source of acceptance and approval, such as great human love, or the love of God.

- When facing the reality of failure, people try to protect themselves with psychological strategies to maintain their self-respect.

- Most people striving to achieve and maintain fame will not succeed, and their attempts to deal with failure damage the possibility of a good life. The fame motive is a pathetic, never-healing affliction—a cancerous growth on the normal human need for acceptance and approval.

Etymology of the Word *Fame*

The English word *fame* comes to us from one of my daughters-in-law who is Greek, and used her Greek/English dictionary for these definitions. (Her maiden name, by the way, is "Perifimos.") to us from the Greek language: from *phanal* "to speak" and *phema* "a voice"; through *fimizo* "I make famous, I spread a rumor", *fimi* "fame, renown", *perifimos* "renowned, famous", and *fimizome* "I am famous"; to the Latin *fama,* from *fari* "to speak". Used as a noun, *fame* means "a report," "a rumor," "news," "the talk of the multitude," as in the following examples: I hear this only from public fame and "At the fame of his approach, the colonists retreated northward."

Fame was used as a verb, as in "to fame" or "He was famed for . . ." It became an adjective and, gradually, "the character attributed to a person or thing by report," that is, a reputation, for example, "It is famed that they were both generals in the emperor of China's armies."

While the verb *to fame* is now rare (if it is used at all), the verb *to defame* is still actively with us. A person can defame another by spreading a report of a character fault or a bad act. Defamation of character, where the report is false, is a basis for legal action against the defamer. The current usage, in fact, means "to injure or endeavor to injure the reputation of another by evil and false reports."

There are synonyms for *fame.* The words that are similar share the meaning that a person is known, spoken about, reported on, perhaps rec-

---

See the etymology of the word *fame* in *The Compact Edition of the Oxford English Dictionary,* 20th ed. (New York: Oxford University Press, 1971).

ognized. But some carry a special meaning of a type or quality of fame, and several refer to the way in which fame was achieved.

Thus *famous* may imply little more than the fact of being, sometimes briefly, widely and popularly known. (In Shakespeare's works, the word *fame* was used eighty-seven times. There was no moral cast as to whether it was good or bad, but the usage leaned in the direction of being a reward for socially valued achievements.) *Renowned* may imply more glory and acclamation. *Celebrated* may mean more notice and attention, especially in print. Still, this is an amorphous category. *Noted* suggests a well-deserved public attention. *Distinguished* implies acknowledged excellence or superiority, while *eminent* implies even greater conspicuousness for outstanding quality or character. For instance, Dean Keith Simonton, in his book *Greatness*, uses a measure of eminence in science that includes having entries in every one of six biographical dictionaries.[1]

Notorious frequently adds to *famous* an implication of questionableness or evil. It refers to someone noted "for some bad practice, quality; unfavorably known; well known on account of something which is not generally approved of or admired; e.g., notorious promiscuity." Beyond *notorious* is *infamous,* "a person of evil report, noted for a bad deed." This is a person "having a reputation of the worst kind; publicly branded with odium for vice . . . ; base; scandalous; notoriously vile;—an infamous liar; an infamous rake or gambler."

What would be the opposite of fame? Is it infamy? No, infamy is one type of fame. The fact is that *fame*—whether being used as a noun, verb, or adjective—has no single sharp antonym. The opposite of fame would be the condition where you are not spoken about or thought about. We have no good word for this condition. *To ignore* seems the opposite of reporting on or speaking about, but it is more than that; it is a deliberate disregard or lack of notice in which case one has been noticed enough to invite ignoring. *Anonymous* might seem the opposite of *famous,* but only in the meaning that one's name is known to only a few or to none, that is, that one is nameless. Many people are famous but anonymous. They have a famous face, voice, or body—they are talked about—but their name is unknown.

Most of the words used as antonyms are negative forms of the synonyms for *fame: inconspicuous, insignificant, unimportant, undistinguished, unknown, unseen, unrecognized, unnoticed. Obscure* and *obscurity* are the best I can do in looking for words without a negative prefix or suffix. Although their basic meaning is "to be without enough light, to be in the dark, to not be able to be seen," it has come to include the very adjectives just mentioned—*unknown, unnoticed.* It applies to persons not illustrious or noted, humble, lowly, and mean—to "a state of being unknown to fame," as in the following examples.

- My fameless name is doomed to oblivion.
- Earth's unknown heroes sink to a fameless grave.

What Kind of Famous Person
Would You Most Like to Be?

A survey entitled "What Kind of Famous Person Would You Most Like to Be?" was conducted by the Roper Organization in February 1987 (Roper Report 87-3, February 14–28) and repeated in February 1993 and March 1997. Respondents were asked the following question:

> Here is a list of some different kinds of famous people. *(Card shown respondent)* Which one or two of those famous types would you most like to be?

The following table lists the percentage of respondents choosing each type of fame, from greatest to least.

	1997	*1993*	*1987*
An author of best-selling books	14	13	15
A popular singer	11	17	15
A sports star in a team sport (basketball, football, baseball, etc.)	11	10	14
A movie actor or actress	10	13	11
A high-ranking businessman	10	9	13
A pianist, trumpet player, violinist, etc.	7	9	14
A famous artist	7	8	11

	1997	*1993*	*1987*
A sports star where you play on your own (tennis, golf, etc.)	6	4	6
A TV star	5	6	5
A famous journalist or newscaster	5	5	5
A famous scientist	5	4	7
A high-ranking government official, like mayor, governor, senator, cabinet officer, etc.	4	7	7
An astronaut	4	3	7
A stage actor or actress	2	2	2
An opera singer	1	2	2
None of these	31	25	18
Don't know	4	7	3

German and Beijing Surveys

In 2002, a German telephone survey of 2,004 persons was directed by the Max Planck Institute for Human Development in Berlin, Germany. The respondents were a random sample representative of the residential adult population, aged eighteen years or older. A Beijing telephone survey was carried out by the Research Center for Contemporary China at Peking University in Beijing. It was included as part of the Beijing Area Study (BAS), an extensive survey of the Beijing population conducted annually by the center.

The Beijing study of fame follows the sampling design of the BAS 2001. The target population of the BAS is comprised of adults who (1) are between ages eighteen and sixty-five, (2) dwell in family households, (3) are formally registered in nonagricultural households, and (4) currently live in resident dwellings in the urban areas of Beijing (i.e., the four inner-city districts and the urban sections of the four suburban districts). The study of fame used the existing sample of BAS 2001 and was based on those respondents of BAS 2001 who reported phone numbers. There were 424 completed interviews out of 615 target respondents. Of the 168 nonresponses, 101 were "no contacts" due to a wrong number or no answer after numerous calls, and 67 were beeper or cell phone numbers that never replied to our call. However, there was no refusal when the contact was established.

In the German and the Beijing surveys and in two comparable U.S. surveys, a decade apart (described in chapter 2), respondents were first asked,

It has been said that eventually everyone will get their fifteen minutes of fame, that is, be well known or widely recognized for an accomplishment or activity for a short period of time. How likely do you think [it is that] this will really happen to you?

The results (in percentages of respondents) were

	United States	Germany	Beijing
Very Likely	14	17	5
Somewhat Likely	17	31	40
Combined	31	48	45

Respondents were then asked,

Most people at some time or another daydream about what it would be like if they were famous. Have you ever daydreamed about being famous?

The percentage of respondents saying yes were

United States	Germany	Beijing
52/57	31	31

The U.S. responses are from two different polls a decade apart.

Fame in Different Languages

As is evident from my note about Greek and Latin in "Etymology of the Word *Fame*," languages have many words describing variations in the substance of fame, nuances in the meaning of being famous. Examples include the following:

Albanian	*famë, emër, nam, reputacion*
Arabic	*dafiʾ ash-shuhra* (when an act is motivated by a wish to achieve fame)
Czech	*sláva*
French	*renommée, gloire*
German	*Ruhm, Berühmtheit, Bekanntheit, guter Ruf*
Hungarian	*hírnévre tesz szert*
Indonesian	*masyhur*
Norwegian	*berømmelse, ry*
Persian	*âvâze, nâmvari, xosrovi*
Polish	*sława, rozglos, imię, renoma*
Portuguese	*fama, renome, honra, nome*
Romanian	*glorie, renume, nume, celebritate, cinste*
Serbo-Croatian	*slava*
Slovak	*sláva, povesť*
Spanish	*fama, gloria, conocimiento*
Swahili	*adhama, adhima, fahar, jaha, taadhima, umaarufu, utukufu*

Swedish	*berömmelse, ryktbarhet, rykte, anseende*
Thai	*chue siang, kittisup, leung lue*
Tibetan	*skad grags, skad sgra che, grags can, snyan grags, snyan grags can, snyan dar, gtam grags*
Turkish	*şohret, ün, ad, nam, söylenti, rivayet, san*
Yiddish	*barimtkeit, schem*

Further examples may be found through multiple online translation dictionaries, such as Word2Word.com, freedict.com, and YourDictionary .com.

Guinness Book of Records

During the last several years, the *Guinness Book of Records* has been published in the following languages:

Arabic	French	Norwegian
Bulgarian	German	Polish
Chinese	Greek	Portuguese
Croatian	Hebrew	Romanian
Czech	Hungarian	Russian
Danish	Italian	Slovenian
Dutch	Japanese	Spanish
English	Korean	Swedish
Finnish	Macedonian	

It is regularly sold in the following countries:

Algeria	Canada	France	Israel
Argentina	Chile	Georgia	Italy
Australia	China	Germany	Kenya
Austria	Colombia	Ghana	Japan
Bangladesh	Croatia	Greece	Latvia
Belgium	Czech Republic	Holland	Lithuania
Bosnia	Denmark	Hungary	Luxemburg
Botswana	Egypt	India	Macedonia
Bulgaria	Finland	Ireland	Malaysia

Mexico	Peru	South Korea	United Arab Emirates
Morocco	Poland	Spain	United Kingdom
New Zealand	Portugal	Sri Lanka	United States
Nigeria	Romania	Sweden	Uruguay
Norway	Russia	Switzerland	Venezuela
Pakistan	Singapore	Taiwan	Zimbabwe
Palestine	Slovakia	Tunisia	
Panama	South Africa	Ukraine	

Gender, Age, and Education Differences

This section presents data compiled from the U.S., German, and Beijing surveys discussed in chapter 2 (see also "German and Beijing Surveys"). Responses to the survey questions are categorized by the respondents' gender, age, and education and are given in percentages.

Gender

"It has been said that eventually everyone will get their fifteen minutes of fame, that is, be well known or widely recognized for an accomplishment or activity for a short period of time. How likely do you think [it is that] this will really happen to you?"

In this table and in the others that follow, in addition to the "very likely" "somewhat likely" percentages, I present the combined figure because of the small percentages—3 and 7 percent—for the Beijing respondents. These seem to be low because of the Chinese word used for "very likely," which may be more extreme in describing the chances of becoming famous. Either way, the separate and combined figures are of interest.

United States	Female	Male
Very Likely	10	17
Somewhat Likely	18	17
Combined	28	34

Germany	Female	Male
Very Likely	15	19
Somewhat Likely	27	34
Combined	42	53

Beijing	Female	Male
Very Likely	3	7
Somewhat Likely	37	43
Combined	40	50

"Most people at some time or another daydream about what it would be like if they were famous. Have you ever daydreamed about being famous?"

United States	Female	Male
1987 poll: Yes	55	59
1997 poll: Yes	50	54

Germany	Female	Male
Yes	27	35

Beijing	Female	Male
Yes	29	32

"Most people spend at least a small part of their waking hours daydreaming and thinking about different things. Some of those daydreams may be complete flights of fancy, others just simple, like a hungry person thinking about lunchtime. Here's a list of some things people might be expected to daydream about from time to time. Could you look it over and call off the things, if any, that you ever daydream or think about?"
(Data available only for the United States.)

United States	Female	Male
1979 poll: Yes	13	24
1984 poll: Yes	14	22

Age

"It has been said that eventually everyone will get their fifteen minutes of fame, that is, be well known or widely recognized for an accomplishment or activity for a short period of time. How likely do you think [it is that] this will really happen to you?"

United States	*18–24*	*25–29*	*30–39*	*40–49*	*50–64*	*65+*
Very Likely	15	24	13	15	11	8
Somewhat Likely	29	35	19	16	9	8
Combined	44	59	32	31	20	14

Germany						
Very Likely	18	24	7	15	18	14
Somewhat Likely	48	41	41	34	21	31
Combined	66	65	58	49	39	45

Beijing	*18–29*		*50–67*	
Very Likely	9	4	35	4
Somewhat Likely	52	43	35	34
Combined	61	47	38	38

"Most people at some time or another daydream about what it would be like if they were famous. Have you ever daydreamed about being famous?"

United States	*18–29*	*30–44*	*45–59*	*60*
1987 poll: Yes	75	61	48	36
1997 poll: Yes	67	57	46	34

Germany				
Yes	54	39	25	15

Beijing				
Yes	50	30	26	23

"Most people spend at least a small part of their waking hours daydreaming and thinking about different things. Some of those daydreams may be complete flights of fancy, others just simple, like a hungry person thinking about lunchtime. Here's a list of some things people might be expected to daydream about from time to time. Could you look it over and call off the things, if any, that you ever daydream or think about?"

(Data available only for the United States.)

United States	*18–29*	*30–44*	*45–59*	*60+*
1979 poll: Yes	31	17	11	8
1984 poll: Yes	31	20	10	4

Education

"It has been said that eventually everyone will get their fifteen minutes of fame, that is, be well known or widely recognized for an accomplishment or activity for a short period of time. How likely do you think [it is that] this will happen to you?"

United States	*Less than* *High School*	*Some* *College*	*College* *Graduate*	*Postgraduate*
Very Likely	8	18	16	21
Somewhat Likely	15	17	21	23
Combined	21	35	37	44

Germany	*Grade 9* *Graduate*	*Grade 10* *Graduate*	*Grade 12/13* *Graduate*	*University* *Graduate*
Very Likely	15	15	19	22
Somewhat Likely	22	34	39	31
Combined	37	49	58	53

Beijing	*Illiterate/Primary* *School Completed/* *Junior High* *School Completed*	*Senior* *High* *School* *Completed*	*College* *Completed*	*University* *Completed/* *Master's Degree/* *Doctorate Degree*
Very Likely	3	3	7	13
Somewhat Likely	31	45	48	43
Combined	34	48	55	56

"Most people at some time or another daydream about what it would be like if they were famous. Have you ever daydreamed about being famous?"

United States	Less than High School	High School Graduate	Some College	College Graduate
1987 poll: Yes	47	54	—	66
1997 poll: Yes	44	53	55	51

Germany	Grade 9 Graduate	Grade 10 Graduate	Grade 12/13 Graduate	University Graduate
Yes	19	32	47	40

Beijing	Illiterate/Primary School Completed/ Junior High School Completed	Senior High School Completed	College Completed	University Completed/ Master's Degree/ Doctorate Degree
Yes	26	34	42	26

"Most people spend at least a small part of their waking hours daydreaming and thinking about different things. Some of those daydreams may be complete flights of fancy, others just simple, like a hungry person thinking about lunchtime. Here's a list of some things people might be expected to daydream about from time to time. Could you look it over and call off the things, if any, that you ever daydream or think about?"

(Data available only for the United States.)

United States	Less than High School	High School Graduate	Some College	College Graduate
1979 poll: Yes	11	15	—	24
1984 poll: Yes	10	17	—	25

Preferred Uses of Fame

A national opinion poll conducted in 2000 by Louis Harris and Associates (no. 43, August 9, 2000) asked respondents, "If you were famous, how would you be likely to use your fame?" The results (in percentages of respondents) follow.

	Very Likely	Somewhat Likely
To help others who are less fortunate than you are.	84	12
To help make a business, organization, product, or service better known.	48	28
To help get a promotion at work or find a better job.	37	19
To help make more people be aware of your talents, abilities, or expertise.	35	30
To promote your personal or career accomplishments.	30	25

Notes

INTRODUCTION

1. On how to become famous, see E. Segal, *Getting Your Fifteen Minutes of Fame—and More! A Guide to Guaranteeing Your Business Success* (New York: Wiley, 2000); G. Rubin, *Power, Money, Fame, Sex: A User's Guide* (New York: Pocketbooks, 2000). For descriptions about famous people, see C. James, *Fame in the 20th century* (New York: Random House, 1993). Regarding fame through the ages, see L. Braudy, *The Frenzy of Renown: Fame and Its History* (New York: Oxford University Press, 1986). For a sociological analysis of prestige, see W. J. Goode, *The Celebration of Heroes: Prestige as a Social Control System* (Berkeley: University of California Press, 1978). Economic analysis of the value of fame is treated in T. Cowen, *What Price Fame?* (Cambridge, MA: Harvard University Press, 2000). See also E. Healey, *Wives of Fame* (Anstey, Leicestershire: Thorpe, 1986); M. Forbes and J. Bloch, *What Happened to Their Kids: Children of the Rich and Famous* (New York: Simon and Schuster, 1990); J. Stewart, *Naked Pictures of Famous People* (New York: Rob Weisbach Books, 1998); I. Wallace, A. Wallace, D. Wallechinsky, and S. Wallace, *The Intimate Sex Lives of Famous People* (New York: Delacorte, 1981); M. Forbes, *They Went That-a-way: How the Famous, the Infamous, and the Great Died* (New York: Ballantine Books, 1999); D. Cross and R. Bent, *Dead Ends: An Irreverent Field Guide to the Graves of the Famous* (New York: Plume, 1991).

2. R. K. Merton, ed., *The Sociology of Science: Theoretical and Empirical Investigations* (Chicago: University of Chicago Press, 1973).

3. J. C. Hermanowicz, *The Stars Are Not Enough: Scientists—Their Passions and Professions* (Chicago: University of Chicago Press, 1998).

CHAPTER 1

1. W. James, *The Principles of Psychology* (New York: Henry Holt, 1890).

2. H. A. Murray, *Explorations in Personality* (New York: Oxford University Press, 1938).

3. R. F. Baumiester and M. R. Leary, "The Need to Belong: Desire for Interpersonal Attachments as a Fundamental Human Motivation," *Psychological Bulletin* 117 (1995), reprinted in *Motivational Science: Social and Personality Perspectives,* ed. E. T. Higgins and R. W. Kruglanski (Philadelphia: Taylor and Francis, 2000). See also J. T. Cacioppo and B. Patrick, *Loneliness: Human Nature and the Need for Social Connection* (New York: W. W. Norton, 2008).

4. Many treatments of the learned component affecting acceptance and approval are in J. Cassidy and P. R. Shaver, eds., *Handbook of Attachment Theory and Research* (New York: Guilford, 1999). On outcomes of rejection and social exclusion, see M. A. Hofer, "Psychobiological Roots of Early Attachment," *Current Directions in Psychological Science* 15, no. 2 (2006); G. Posada and A. Jacobs, "Child-Mother Attachment Relationships and Culture," *American Psychologist* 56, no. 10 (2002); K. D. Williams, J. P. Forgas, and W. Von Hippel, eds., *The Social Outcast: Ostracism, Social Exclusion, Rejection, and Bullying* (Sydney: University of New South Wales, 2005).

5. S. Freud, "The Psychogenesis of a Case of Homosexuality in a Woman," in *The Standard Edition of the Complete Psychological Works of Sigmund Freud,* ed. and trans. J. Strachey, vol. 18 (London: Hogarth, 1955).

6. S. Bloland, "Fame: The Power and Cost of a Fantasy," *Atlantic Monthly,* November 1999.

7. J. M. Adler, "Fame, Narcissism, and Self-Complexity in Fans and Celebrities" (Dissertation, Bates College, 2000). Also on this topic, see L. Layton, "Who's That Girl? A Case Study of Madonna," in *Women Creating Lives: Identities, Resilience, and Resistance,* ed. C. E. Franz and A. J. Stewart (Boulder: Westview, 1994), 143–57.

8. Joyce Wadler, "A Defiant Jester, Laughing Best," *New York Times,* July 27, 2006.

9. J. Macur, "There's Terrell and There's T.O., and They Unite in Midstride," *New York Times,* November 28, 2004.

10. W. Koestenbaum, *Andy Warhol* (New York: Viking, 2001).

11. K. Butler, "Beyond Rivalry, a Hidden World of Sibling Violence," *New York Times,* February 28, 2006.

12. E. Goode, "School Bullying Is Common, Mostly by Boys, Study Finds," *New York Times,* April 25, 2001.

13. N. Gibbs and T. Roche, "The Columbine Tapes," *Time,* December 20, 1999.

14. N. S. Kleinfield, "Before Deadly Rage, a Lifetime Consumed by a Troubling Silence," *New York Times,* April 22, 2007.

15. Harris Survey, no. 893003, September 1989.

16. An interesting study of images was conducted by the Roper Organization, in the Roper Reports series in February 1987, February 1993, and March 1997.

17. S. Bloland, *In the Shadow of Fame: A Memoir by the Daughter of Erik H. Erikson* (New York: Viking, 2005).

CHAPTER 2

1. *USA Today,* December 1985. Gordon S. Black, *PM Magazine.*

2. Research and Forecasts Survey, "Working Americans: Emerging Values," October 1988.

3. Peter D. Hart Research Associates, "Men's Life Survey of Men," May 1990; Luntz Research Companies, "*Wired/*Merrill Lynch Forum Digital Citizen Survey," October 1997.

4. *Los Angeles Times,* December 16, 1989.

5. Roper Organization, Roper Report 75-7, September 1975; 1985.

6. *Year 2000 Census,* table 1, available at http://www.census.gov/population/socdemo/age/p20-532/tab01.txt.

7. For health statistics about noninstitutionalized populations in the United States, see U.S. Department of Health and Human Services, Centers for Disease Control and Prevention, National Center for Health Statistics, *Summary Health Statistics for U.S. Adults: National Health Interview Survey, 2002,* Vital and Health Statistics, series 10, no. 222, DHHS publication no. (PHS) 2004-1550 (Hyattsville, MD: U.S. Department of Health and Human Services, 2004).

8. Pew Research Center, Generation Next Survey, USSRBI.010907 P.R12, September 2006.

9. American Psychiatric Association, *Diagnostic and Statistical Manual of Mental Disorders,* 4th ed. (Washington, DC: American Psychiatric Association, 1994).

10. Roper Organization, Roper Report 87-3, May 1987; 1993; 1997.

11. Roper Organization, Roper Report 84-3, April 1984; 1979; 1989; 1992; 1997.

12. Louis Harris and Associates, no. 43, August 9, 2000.

13. About one-third of respondents answered that it is desirable or important to be famous in a February 1987 survey by the Roper Organization entitled "The American Dream."

14. Survey by Louis Harris and Associates, July 17–July 21, 1998, available at iPOLL Databank, Roper Center for Public Opinion Research, University of Connecticut, http://www.ropercenter.uconn.edu/ipoll.html (accessed December 3, 2008).

15. Survey by Wall Street Journal and Roper Organization, October 1986, available at iPOLL Databank, Roper Center for Public Opinion Research, University of Connecticut, http://www.ropercenter.uconn.edu/ipoll.html (accessed December 3, 2008).

16. Survey by Barna Research Group, July 1993, available at iPOLL Databank, Roper Center for Public Opinion Research, University of Connecticut, http://www.roperenter.uconn.edu/ipoll.html (accessed December 3, 2008).

17. Survey by Barna Research Group, January 1991, available at iPOLL Databank, Roper Center for Public Opinion Research, University of Connecticut, http://www.ropercenter.uconn.edu/ipoll.html (accessed December 3, 2008).

18. Survey by Shearson Lehman Brothers and Roper Organization, May 1992, available at iPOLL Databank, Roper Center for Public Opinion Research, University of Connecticut, http://www.ropercenter.uconn.edu/ipoll.html (accessed December 3, 2008).

19. S. Scheibe, A. Freund, and P. Baltes, *Toward a Psychology of Lifespan-Longing: Conceptualization, Measurement, and Correlates with Psychological Well-Being* (Berlin: Max Planck Institute for Human Development).

20. "Questionable Paths to Fame," *Shanghai Star,* January 2, 2003, http://appl .chinadaily.com.cn/star/2003/0102/vo2-3.html (accessed January 14, 2009).

21. O. Standing, "Barefoot on the Golden Silvery Sands," in *Welcome to Sri Lanka and Colombo* (Colombo, Sri Lanka: Crystal, 2003).

22. *Guinness World Records 2000* (New York: Bantam Books, 2000).

23. Additional treatment of our ignorance about what it is we really want in life is found in G. Brim, *Ambition: How We Manage Success and Failure throughout Our Lives* (New York: Basic Books, 1992; reprint, Authors Guild Backinprint.com ed., Lincoln, NE: iUniverse, 2000).

CHAPTER 3

1. *Barbara Walters Special,* ABC, April 26, 1995.

2. G. Rubin, *Power, Money, Fame, Sex: A User's Guide* (New York: Pocketbooks, 2000).

3. Aguilera's interview is reported in L. L. Torregrosa, "At 18, Singer Seeks to Prove She's Not a One-Hit Wonder," *New York Times,* September 6, 1999.

4. L. Belkin, "Death on the CNN Curve," *New York Times Magazine,* July 23, 1995.

5. Harris and Associates, "Mood Leaders," July 17–21, 1998.

6. E. Lemert, *Human Deviance, Social Problems, and Social Control* (Englewood Cliffs, NJ: Prentice-Hall, 1972).

7. L. Braudy, *The Frenzy of Renown: Fame and Its History* (New York: Oxford University Press, 1986).

8. H. Zuckerman, *Scientific Elite: Nobel Laureates in the United States* (New York: Free Press, 1977).

9. See O. G. Brim and S. Wheeler, *Socialization after childhood: Two essays* (New York: Wiley, 1966).

10. C. Murphy, "In Darkest Academia: Publish a Best-Seller and Perish," *Harper's Magazine,* October 1978.

11. D. A. Hollinger, "Star Power," review of *Carl Sagan: A Life,* by Keay Davidson, and *Carl Sagan: A Life In the Cosmos,* by William Poundstone, *New York Times Book Review,* November 28, 1999.

12. P. Fara, "Face Values: How Portraits Win Friends and Influence People," *Science* 299 (February 7, 2003).

13. Alfred, Lord Tennyson, "Merlin and Vivien," in *Idylls of the King* (1863),

available at http://www.everypoet.com/archive/poetry/Tennyson/tennyson_contents _idylls_merlin_and_vivien.htm (accessed April 21, 2007).

CHAPTER 4

1. B. Schulberg, *What Makes Sammy Run* (New York: Random House, 1952).

2. P. David Marshall, *Celebrity and Power: Fame in Contemporary Culture* (Minneapolis: University of Minnesota Press, 1997).

3. J. S. Mill, *Utilitarianism* (1863), chap. 4, available at http://www.utilitarian ism.org/mill4.htm (accessed March 30, 2000).

4. D. McClelland, *Human Motivation* (New York: Cambridge University Press, 1987).

5. A. H. Maslow, *Motivation and Personality,* rev. ed. (New York: Harper and Row, 1970); C. Jung, "The Stages of Life" (1930), reprinted in *The Portable Jung* (New York: Viking, 1961); K. Horney, *Neurosis and Human Growth: The Struggle toward Self-Realization* (New York: Norton, 1950); E. Fromm, *Escape from Freedom* (New York: Holt, Rinehart, and Winston, 1941; reprint, New York: Avon Books, 1965). The definition of individuality is found in *Webster's New Universal Unabridged Dictionary,* 2nd ed. (New York: Simon and Schuster, 1979).

6. C. Snyder and H. Franken, *The Human Pursuit of Difference* (New York: Plenum, 1982). Also see C. Snyder and S. Lopez, eds., *Handbook of Positive Psychology* (New York: Oxford University Press, 2002).

7. The Swedish Twin Registry was reported by G. McClearn, personal communication, May 1987.

8. Snyder and Franken, *Human Pursuit of Difference.*

9. American Psychiatric Association, *Diagnostic and Statistical Manual of Mental Disorders,* 4th ed. (Washington, DC: American Psychiatric Association, 1994).

10. T. Millon, "The Disorders of Personality," in *Handbook of Personality: Theory and Research,* ed. L. A. Pervin (New York: Guilford, 1990).

11. S. Young and D. Pinsky, "Narcissism and Celebrity," *Journal of Research and Personality* 40 (2006).

12. American Psychiatric Association, *Diagnostic and Statistical Manual.*

13. J. Atkinson, R. Heyns, and J. Veroff, "The Effect of Experimental Arousal of the Affiliation Motive on Thematic Apperception," *Journal of Abnormal and Social Psychology* 49 (1954).

INTRODUCTION TO PART 2

1. Samuel Johnson, *Rambler* no. 146 (August 10, 1751), available at http://www .samueljohnson.com/fame.html (accessed October 13, 2003).

2. See O. G. Brim and Carol D. Ryff, "On the Properties of Life Events," in *Life-Span Development and Behavior,* ed. P. B. Baltes and O. G. Brim (New York: Academic Press, 1980).

3. G. Brim, *Ambition: How We Manage Success and Failure throughout Our Lives* (New York: Basic Books, 1992; reprint, Authors Guild Backinprint.com ed., Lincoln, NE: iUniverse, 2000). Also see G. Brim and J. Kagan, eds., *Constancy and Change in Human Development* (Cambridge, MA: Harvard University Press, 1980).

4. O. P. John, "The 'Big Five' Factor Taxonomy: Dimensions of Personality in the Natural Language and in Questionnaires," in *Handbook of Personality: Theory and Research,* ed. L. A. Pervin (New York: Guilford, 1990).

5. M. E. P. Seligman, *What You Can Change and What You Can't* (Columbine, NY: Fawcett, 1993).

CHAPTER 5

1. L. Braudy, *The Frenzy of Renown: Fame and Its History* (New York: Oxford University Press, 1986).

2. J. Ball and J. Jonnes, *Fame at Last: Who Was Who according to the* New York Times *Obituaries* (Kansas City, MO: Andrews McMeel, 2000).

3. D. Wallechinsky and A. Wallace, *The Book of Lists* (New York: Canongate Books, 2005).

4. A. Schopenhauer, *The Wisdom of Life and Other Essays: The Works of Arthur Schopenhauer* (Whitefish, MT: Kessinger, 2004).

5. See T. Cowen, *What Price Fame?* (Cambridge, MA: Harvard University Press, 2000).

6. See D. Roberts, *True Summit: What Really Happened on the Legendary Ascent of Annapurna* (New York: Touchstone, 2000).

7. C. James, *Fame in the 20th Century* (New York: Random House, 1993).

8. Braudy, *The Frenzy of Renown: Fame and Its History.*

9. W. Goode, *The Celebration of Heroes: Prestige as a Social Control System* (Berkeley: University of California Press, 1978).

10. J. English, *The Economy of Prestige* (Cambridge, MA: Harvard University Press, 2005).

11. E. Segal, *Getting Your Fifteen Minutes of Fame—and More! A Guide to Guaranteeing Your Business Success* (New York: Wiley, 2000).

12. G. Easterbrook, "Forgotten Benefactor of Humanity," *Atlantic Monthly,* January 1999.

13. L. Lapham, "Philosopher Kings," *Harper's Magazine,* October 2001.

14. R. Huber, *The American Idea of Success* (New York: McGraw-Hill, 1971).

15. Cowen, *What Price Fame?*

16. G. Hellinga, "Fame as a Guiding Fiction," *Journal of Individual Psychology* 31, no. 2 (November 1975).

17. Braudy, *Frenzy of Renown.*

18. *Roget's International Thesaurus,* 4th ed., revised by Robert L. Chapman (New York: Harper and Row, 1977), 675.2–675.12.

19. J. Milton, *Samson Agonistes* (1671), line 971.

20. Goode, *Celebration of Heroes.*

21. Ball and Jonnes, *Fame at Last.*

22. Braudy, *Frenzy of Renown.*

23. Jim Rutenberg, "Reality Television Strikes a Stark Note in a New Show," *New York Times,* August 21, 2000.

24. J. Bradley, *Flags of Our Fathers.* New York: Bantam Books, 2000.

25. "Widows Stage Protest on Bhopal Anniversary," *Vero Beach Press Journal,* December 4, 1994.

26. R. Goldstein, "Al Smith, 73, Who Got Beer Bath in World Series, Dies," *New York Times,* January 6, 2002.

27. I. Berkow, "The Most Infamous Seat in the House: Memories of a Fan's Misplay Die Hard in Wrigley Field," *New York Times,* September 10, 2004.

CHAPTER 6

1. Salmon Rushdie is quoted in *Modern Maturity,* July/August 1999.

2. Louis Harris and Associates, "Mood Leaders," July 17, 1998.

3. Hazlitt is quoted in G. Rubin, *Power, Money, Fame, Sex: A User's Guide* (New York: Pocketbooks, 2000).

4. A. Pope, *The Temple of Fame* (1716), line 523.

5. G. Brim, *Ambition: How We Manage Success and Failure throughout Our Lives* (New York: Basic Books, 1992; reprint, Authors Guild Backinprint.com ed., Lincoln, NE: iUniverse, 2000).

6. Roper Organization, "Values," May 16–May 30, 1987.

7. Hixson is quoted in E. Culotta, "Science's 20 Greatest Hits Take Their Lumps," *Science* 251 (March 15, 1991).

8. C. Conner and P. Chronis, "Fame Motive for Juror?" *Denver Post,* April 12, 2002.

9. N. Franklin, "Childhood, Inc." *New Yorker,* April 19, 2004.

10. *Living Dolls: The Making of a Child Beauty Queen,* HBO, May 13, 2001.

11. F. Grimm, "John Kerry Was YouTubed, Bro, for Show," *Miami Herald,* September 20, 2007, http://www.miamiherald.com/news/columnists/fred_grimm/v-print/story/243786.htm (accessed September 20, 2007).

12. A. Jacobs, "A Caped Crusader for Peace (and Fun)," *New York Times,* October 9, 2004.

13. *The Compact Edition of the Oxford English Dictionary,* 20th printing, vol. 2 (New York: Oxford University Press, 1971).

14. See J. Gamson, *Claims to Fame: Celebrity in Contemporary America* (Berkeley, CA: University of California Press, 1994); D. Boorstin, *The Image: A Guide to Pseudo-Events in America* (New York: Harper and Row, 1961).

15. J. Gamson, "Celebrity," in *International Encyclopedia of the Social and Behavioral Sciences,* ed. N. Smelser and P. Baltes (New York: Elsevier, 2001).

16. D. Giles, *Illusions of Immortality: A Psychology of Fame and Celebrity* (New York: St. Martin's, 2000).

17. S. Klein, "Reader, I Dated Him," *New York Times,* July 24, 2005.

18. *Guinness World Records 2000* (New York: Bantam Books, 2000).

19. *It Should Happen To You* (Columbia Pictures, 1954).

20. Judy Holliday Resource Center, *It Should Happen to You*, "About the Film," http://www.wtv-zone.com/lumina/films/it.html (accessed June 10, 2007).

21. M. de Cervantes, *Don Quixote de la Mancha* (New York: Oxford University Press, 1992).

22. W. J. Goode, *The Celebration of Heroes: Prestige as a Social Control System* (Berkeley: University of California Press, 1978).

23. Cervantes, *Don Quixote.*

24. Sutcliffe, http://www.communitypolicing.org/publications/comlinks/cl_9/c8_sutcl.htm.

25. See R. Schickel, *Intimate Strangers: The Culture of Celebrity* (New York: Fromm International, 1986).

26. M. Orth, *The Importance of Being Famous: Behind the Scenes of the Celebrity-Industrial Complex* (New York: Henry Holt, 2004).

27. J. Oates, "I Had No Other Thrill or Happiness," *New York Review of Books*, March 24, 1994.

28. See C. James, *Fame in the 20th Century* (New York: Random House, 1993).

CHAPTER 7

1. Erving Goffman, *The Presentation of Self in Everyday Life* (New York: Doubleday, 1959).

2. S. K. Scher, ed., *The Currency of Fame: Portrait Medals of the Renaissance* (New York: Harry N. Abrams, 1994).

3. F. Allen, *Treadmill to Oblivion* (Boston: Little, Brown, 1954).

4. T. Lawson and A. Parsons, *The Magic behind the Voices: A Who's Who of Cartoon Voice Actors* (Jackson: University Press of Mississippi, 2004).

CHAPTER 8

1. R. Schickel, *Intimate Strangers: The Culture of Celebrity* (New York: Fromm International, 1986).

2. T. Dreiser, *Sister Carrie* (New York: Doubleday, Page, 1900).

3. J. C. Hermanowicz, *The Stars Are Not Enough: Scientists—Their Passions and Professions* (Chicago: University of Chicago Press, 1998).

4. L. Braudy, *The Frenzy of Renown: Fame and Its History* (New York: Oxford University Press, 1986).

5. R. Rubin, "The Mall of Fame," *Atlantic Monthly*, July 1977.

6. C. James, *Fame in the 20th Century* (New York: Random House, 1993).

7. "What Is Paradise without Praise?" *New York Times*, April 1, 1997. See also E. Gargan, "For Arthur C. Clarke, Sri Lanka Is a Link to Space," *New York Times*, April 7, 1993.

8. N. Hawthorne, introduction to *The Scarlet Letter* (New York: Random House, 1950).

9. *New Yorker*, December 6, 1999.

10. *Webster's Ninth New Collegiate Dictionary* (Springfield, MA: Merriam-Webster, 1983).

CHAPTER 9

1. D. Simonton, "Age and Outstanding Achievement: What Do We Know after a Century of Research?" *Psychological Bulletin* 104, no. 2 (1988).

2. For discussion of performance by field, see G. Brim, *Ambition: How We Manage Success and Failure throughout Our Lives* (New York: Basic Books, 1992; reprint, Authors Guild Backinprint.com ed., Lincoln, NE: iUniverse, 2000).

3. M. Gross, "Carrie Fisher, Novelist, Looks Back at the Edge," *New York Times*, August 14, 1987.

4. J. London, "The Sun-Dog Trail," *Harpers Magazine*, February 2000.

5. R. Lombreglia, "The Only People for Him," *Atlantic Monthly*, August 1996.

6. A. De Dominicus and B. Johnson, "Alberto Moravia," in *Writers at Work: The* Paris Review *Interviews*, ed. M. Cowley, 1st series (New York: Viking, 1967).

7. D. Giles, *Illusions of Immortality* (New York: St. Martin's, 2000).

8. Brim, *Ambition*.

9. F. Harris, *Contemporary Portraits*, 3rd series (Mellwood, NY: Reprints and Periodicals, Division of Kraus Organization, 1920).

10. A. Schopenhauer, *The Wisdom of Life and Other Essays: The Works of Arthur Schopenhauer* (Whitefish, MT: Kessinger, 2004).

11. See R. Wilson, *The American Poet: A Role Investigation* (New York: Garland, 1990).

12. F. Westie, "Academic Expectations for Professional Immortality: A Study of Legitimation," *Sociological Forum*, Summer 1972.

13. L. Braudy, *The Frenzy of Renown: Fame and Its History* (New York: Oxford University Press, 1986).

14. S. Freud, "The History of the Psychoanalytic Movement," in *The Basic Writings of Sigmund Freud*, ed. and trans. A. A. Brill (New York: Random House, 1938).

15. K. Grimwood, *Replay*, ed. D. Rowland (New York: Berkley, 1988).

16. J. Updike, *The Carpentered Hen and Other Tame Creatures* (New York: Harper and Brothers, 1958); I. Shaw, "The Eighty-Yard Run," in *Short Stories: Five Decades* (New York: Dell, 1983).

17. B. Weinraub, "Why No Star Shines as Bright," *New York Times*, April 29, 2001.

18. S. Johnson, *Rambler* no. 21 (May 29, 1750), available at http://www.samueljohnson.com/writing.html (accessed October 20, 2003).

19. H. Zuckerman, *Scientific Elite: Nobel Laureates in the United States* (New York: Free Press, 1977).

20. C. James, "And Now, the 16th Minute of Fame: In the New Rules of Celebrity, Has-beens Qualify," *New York Times,* March 13, 2002.

21. M. Orth, *The Importance of Being Famous: Behind the Scenes of the Celebrity-Industrial Complex* (New York: Henry Holt, 2004).

22. F. Waitzkin, "The Long-Distance Runner," review of *Chasing the Hawk: Looking for My Father, Finding Myself,* by Andrew Sheehan, *New York Times Book Review,* September 23, 2003.

23. C. Sprawson, "Death of a Champion," review of *The Crossing: The Glorious Tragedy of the First Man to Swim the English Channel,* by Kathy Watson, *New York Review of Books,* September 20, 2001.

24. G. Santayana, "The Unknowable" (Herbert Spencer Lecture, Oxford University, 1923), reprinted in *Reading I've Liked,* ed. C. Fadiman (New York: Simon and Schuster, 1943).

25. G. Lang and K. Lang, *Etched in Memory: The Building and Survival of Artistic Reputation* (Urbana: University of Illinois Press, 2001).

26. J. Ball and J. Jonnes, *Fame at Last: Who Was Who according to the* New York Times *Obituaries* (Kansas City, MO: Andrews McMeel, 2000).

27. http://www.marquiswhoswho.com.

28. K. Teltsch, "Wanted: Contributors in Search of Immortality," *New York Times,* June 11, 1993.

29. H. Dobson, "To an Unknown Bust in the British Museum," stanza 6.

30. C. James, *Fame in the 20th Century* (New York: Random House, 1993).

31. Jeremy Bentham's will can be accessed through the University College London's Bentham Project Web site at http://www.ucl.ac.uk/Bentham-Project (accessed June 7, 2007).

32. A. Delbanco, "Melville Has Never Looked Better," *New York Times Book Review,* October 28, 2001.

33. C. McLaren and J. Hyslop, "Grave Revisionism," *Stay Free!* 17 (Summer 2000), http://ibiblio.org/stayfree/archives/17/dead_celebs.html (accessed March 12, 2002).

CHAPTER 10

1. G. Brim, *Ambition: How We Manage Success and Failure throughout Our Lives* (New York: Basic Books, 1992).

2. R. Baumeister, "The Crystalization of Discontent in the Process of Major Life Change," in *Can Personality Change,* ed. T. Hetherton and J. Weinberger (Washington, DC: American Psychological Association, 1994).

3. S. Bok, *Lying: Moral Choice in Public and Private Life* (New York: Random House, 1979). See also S. Bok, *Secrets: On the Ethics of Concealment and Revelation* (New York: Pantheon, 1983).

4. For a discussion of competition for fame, see Brim, *Ambition.*

5. E. Valenstein, *Great and Desperate Cures* (New York: Basic Books, 1986).

6. Brim, *Ambition.*

7. W. James, *The Varieties of Religious Experience: A Study in Human Nature* (1902; reprint, New York: Modern Library).

8. L. Braudy, *The Frenzy of Renown: Fame and Its History* (New York: Oxford University Press, 1986).

9. *The Monastery,* ABC, August 20, 1981.

10. See J. Heckhausen and O. Brim, "Perceived Problems for Self and Others: Self-Protection by Social Downgrading throughout Adulthood," *Psychology and Aging* 12, no. 4 (1997); J. Todd and J. Worell, "Resilience in Low-Income, Employed, African American Women," *Psychology of Women Quarterly* 24 (2000); F. Gibbons, D. Lane, and M. Gerrard et al., "Comparison-Level Preferences after Performance: Is Downward Comparison Theory Still Useful?" *Journal of Personality and Social Psychology* 83, no. 4 (2002).

11. T. Cowen, *What Price Fame?* (Cambridge, MA: Harvard University Press, 2000).

12. *The Compact Edition of the Oxford English Dictionary,* 20th printing, vol. 2 (New York: Oxford University Press, 1971).

13. S. Bloland, *In the Shadow of Fame.*

ETYMOLOGY OF THE WORD *FAME*

1. D. K. Simonton, Greatness: *Who Makes History and Why* (New York: Guilford Press, 1994).